GIUSEPPE BOVINI

RAVENNA

ART AND HISTORY

WITH 131 PICTURES

LONGO PUBLISHER - RAVENNA

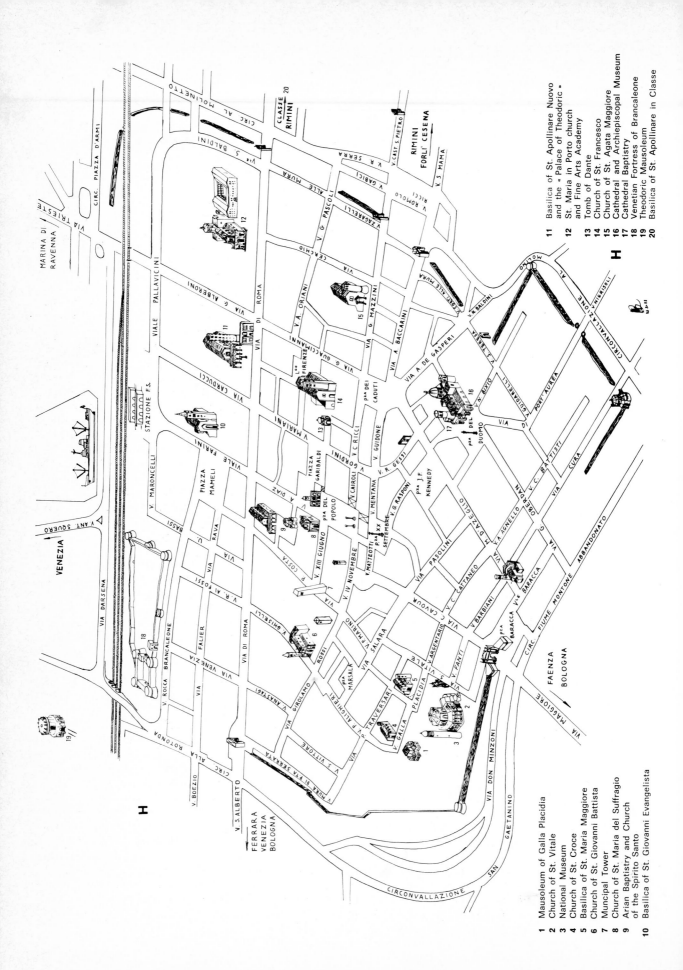

1 Mausoleum of Galla Placidia
2 Church of St. Vitale
3 National Museum
4 Church of St. Croce
5 Basilica of St. Maria Maggiore
6 Church of St. Giovanni Battista
7 Muncipal Tower
8 Church of St. Maria del Suffragio
9 Arian Baptistry and Church
   of the Spirito Santo
10 Basilica of St. Giovanni Evangelista

11 Basilica of St. Apollinare Nuovo
   and the « Palace of Theodoric »
12 St. Maria in Porto church
   and Fine Arts Academy
13 Tomb of Dante
14 Church of St. Francesco
15 Church of St. Agata Maggiore
16 Cathedral and Archiepiscopal Museum
17 Cathedral Baptistry
18 Venetian Fortress of Brancaleone
19 Theodoric Mausoleum
20 Basilica of St. Apollinare in Classe

Today a wide expanse of well cultivated land surrounds Ravenna, but in ancient times the city, which arose upon a group of sand-hills, was washed by the sea and surrounded by marshes. The group of small islands on which the early centre of the city was built, was, however, not entirely isolated, for, north and south, it was connected with that chain of dunes which extended to the delta of the river Po on one side, and on the other to the environs of Cervia.

This long chain of sand-dunes at those times formed a barrier against the sea, but with the passing of the centuries, and the accumulation of alluvional deposits brought down by the various branches of the Po, a new crescent of dunes, marking the limit of the foreshore grew up further eastward, starting from Classe and extending northward.

During the Middle Ages and the centuries that followed the low-lying areas were gradually filled up, so that the sea receded more and more, and the seashore is now nearly 4½ miles from the city.

The early history of Ravenna is lost in the mists of time. Dioniges of Halicarnassus says that the city was founded seven generations before the Trojan War, but we cannot really be sure of this, nor do we know anything of the earliest inhabitants, though Strabo considers that they were of Hellenic descent and had come from Thessaly.

In historic times the city was perhaps inhabited, or rather occupied, for a short period by the Etruscans. This might be deduced not only from the fact that Strabo states that the Thessalonians had to abandon the city as a result of Etruscans attacks, and that they called in the Umbrians before returning to their homes, but more especially from the fact that the suffix -enna seems to be typically Etruscan.

Further evidence of the temporary presence of Etruscans in the city might be assumed from the circumstance that some objects undoubtedly of Etruscan make have been found in Ravenna, for example, some small votive bronzes and a fine statuette of a warrior with an Etruscan inscription, belonging perhaps to the 6th century B.C., now preserved in the Museum of Antiquities at Leyden. But it is obvious that such evidence has no definite value, consisting as it does in small portable objects, for these articles may have been used for purposes of exchange, or may have been imported.

In any case the supposition that Ravenna was once inhabited by Etruscans finds no confirmation in historical tradition, which does, however, lay some stress upon the Umbrians, who, as is well known, pushed their way in historical times from Rimini to the banks of the Po.

We do not know exactly when Rome took possession of the city. It is however certain that after the conquest of the Po Valley by the Romans, Ravenna — which had long been a flourishing centre of commerce — was a strategic bulwark of great importance because of its extraordinary geographical position which made it almost impregnable, for it was on one side separated from the inland regions by the marshes, which constituted an excellent defence, while being at the same time in immediate contact with the open sea, hence it could easily receive reinforcements and supplies.

It is quite possible that Ravenna's first strong urge to maritime development was due to Marius, for Plutarch tells us that the people of Ravenna erected a marble statue of him in his honour. In any case it seems certain that the first Roman fleet to appear at Ravenna was that of Metellus, Sulla's Legate, who disembarked there in 82 B.C.

Two documents of the end of the 12th century mention also a port of Caius Julius Caesar; but it is obvious that the absence of any earlier evidence does not justify (as Torre has rightly observed) any definite statement or conjecture of any kind on this matter. Yet it is probable that Caesar, who chose Ravenna as his headquarters while dealing with the Senate, had, for military reasons, actually carried out some work at the port.

The great development and extension of the port was the work of the Emperor Augustus, who, to defend better the Adriatic and the seas of the near East, decided to make it the base of a pretorian fleet consisting—so Dion Cassius tells us— of 250 ships.

3

Thus about 2½ miles to the south-east of Ravenna arose the Port of Classe, whose vast basin was hollowed out at the very place where the most recently formed range of sand-dunes had become separated from the more ancient chain along the shore.

But the work carried out in Ravenna by the founder of the Empire was not limited to the construction of a great military port. He planned a wide canal which would unite it with the southern branch of the river Po. This was the *Fossa Augusti* mentioned by several writers. Before reaching Ravenna it seems to have been divided into two branches; one surrounded the city walls to assure better defence, the other flowed through the midst of the city thus assisting commercial activity.

In the Augustan era commerce was mainly by water, for Strabo says that in his days the city—where the houses were built upon piles—was intersected by many water-ways regularly swept by the tides which washed out the muddy pools and so kept the air pure. Thus at that time Ravenna, consisting as it did of various islands linked together by numerous bridges, must have presented an altogether remarkable appearance.

Some idea of it—even if not quite corresponding to the truth—may be derived from a graphic reconstruction attempted towards the end of the 17th century by the noted cosmographer of Ravenna, M.V. Coronelli, who, in another design, based especially on information left us by the Arian Bishop Jordanes, tried to show the neighbouring communities of Caesarea and Classe which had developed enormously as a result of having become the permanent station of the great Roman naval fleet.

From that time too Ravenna became familiar with the activities of the shipyards; there is certain proof of this in a funeral pillar (*stele*) *to the faber navalis* i.e. the carpenter of the fleet, Publius Longidienus, who is shown in the act of working with an axe, near an unfinished ship. While the city was growing in size as a result of the increasing population, it was, at the same time, being adorned with fine sculptures.

The three nucleus of Ravenna, Cesarea and Classe: representation by M.V. Coronelli

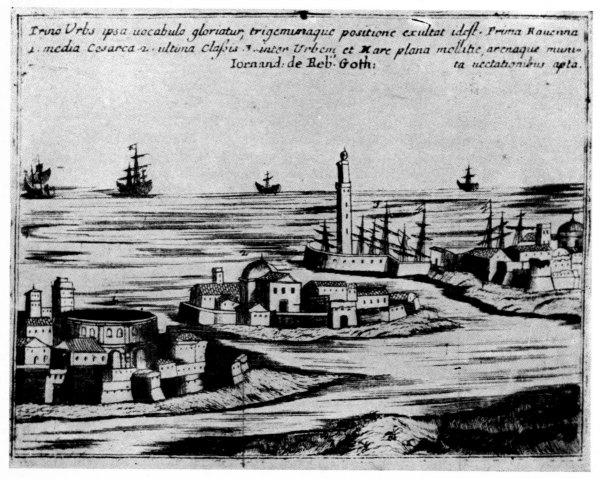

There is the splendid example of the relief to be seen in the National Museum, showing the members of the Julius-Claudian family.

Like other ancient cities Ravenna had a quadrangular perimeter, only the north-east side deviated somewhat from the regularity of the usual plan because of the two waterways all along that side. It is probable also that the nature of the ground did not permit the exact orientation of the *cardo* and the *decumanus* with regards to the four cardinal points. In fact, the two main arteries of the city of Ravenna show an inclination of 45°, one running in the direction SW-NE and the other SE-NW. It is thus not possible to decide with certainty which represented the *cardo* and which the *decumanus*. But as the latter was almost always the wider and more important, it is likely enough that in Ravenna it ran SW-NE for a distance

of about 490 yards, i.e. from the *Porta Aurea* to *the Pons Augustus* (Via Salara).

This being the state of affairs, the *cardo* must have been on the SE-NW axis and must have had at its extremities those two gates which at a later time were called respectively *Porta Salustra and Porta*, or rather *Posterula Latronum*. They opened in the city wall which was built, or a least restored, by the Emperor Claudius in the first year of his reign, 43 A.D.

The *Porta Aurea*, on the contrary, certainly owes its origin to Claudius, for an inscription (of which today a few fragments remain) mentions Tiberius Claudius. This gate, which had two openings, was flanked by two round towers. In fact it is shown thus on the mediaeval seal of the city, and in drawings left by some Renaissance architects, for example those of Palladio and Sangallo. The

Plan of the ancient town of Ravenna, by M.V. Coronelli (end XVIIth cent.)

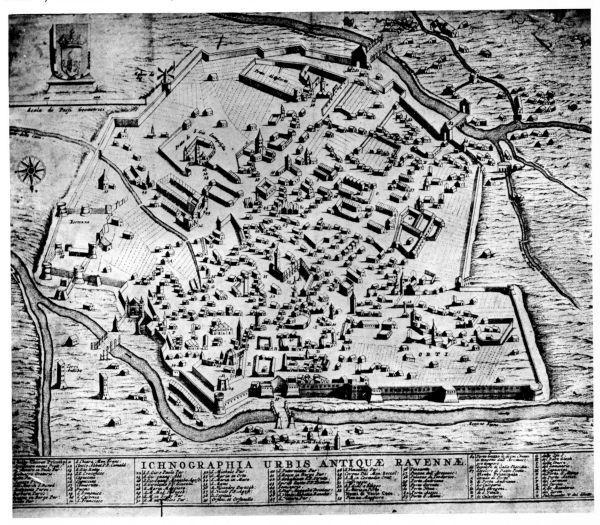

two round towers were thrown down by the Venetians at the end of the 15th century and the gate itself was demolished in 1582 merely to supply building material.

Not far from the Porta Aurea stood the Temple of Apollo and the Amphitheatre, but nothing remains of these, nor of the Circus and the Capitol, of which the latter stood near the present church of St. Dominic.

At the beginning of the 2nd century the Emperor Trajan provided the city with an aqueduct, for Ravenna, as we learn from Martial, was without drinking water; nor can we be surprised at this when we consider the character of the ground and the nearness of the sea.

So water from the Apennines was brought from the region of Teodorano to Ravenna closely following the Ronco, and when the course of this river was diverted, a few piles and arches of the ancient aqueduct were found in its bed not far from the church of S. Bartolomeo in Longana, in the year 1735.

As it grew in importance and in the number of its inhabitants Ravenna grew rapidly in size even before the 2nd century A.D. Buildings began to arise outside the *oppidum* as the old municipal centre was called, in the region which was later called *Regio Caesarum*.

But a still greater expansion took place at the beginning of the 5th century when the Emperor Honorius made Ravenna the Capital of the Empire of the West, in place of Milan. The city then soon lost the appearance of a provincial town and assumed the dignity and grandeur of an imperial residence.

Thus, in the new parts which were added to the inhabited area, magnificent public buildings and superb churches arose, the interiors of which were covered with splendid mosaics; such, for example, were the great Ursian Basilica with its five naves and adjoining Baptistery, the Church of Santa Croce and the so-called Mausoleum of Galla Placidia, the Church of St. John the Evan-

Porta Aurea of Ravenna (drawing by M.V. Coronelli)

gelist, and the church then dedicated to the Apostles, but now to St. Francis.

At the same time the city walls were also extended as a result of the work first of Honorius and Valentinian III, and later by command of Odoacre and Theodoric. With the entrance of Odoacre into Ravenna, and the death of his brother Paul, uncle of Romulus Augustulus, in the pine wood of Classe in 476, the history of the Roman Empire of the West comes to an end. Odoacre was the first of the barbarians to bear the title of King in Italy.

But towards the last decade of the 5th century, preceded by his fame as a conqueror after victories won in battle on the banks of the Isonzo, at Verona, and on the Adda, Theodoric appeared in the neighbourhood of Ravenna at the head of a mighty host of Ostrogoths. After a siege of almost three years, Theodoric, on March 5th, 493, compelled Odoacre—by this time definitely cut off from all possibility of obtaining reinforcements and supplies— to consent to negotiation. It was promised that his life would be spared, and he was given hope that he might retain part of his authority. But ten days later he was accused of treachery and slain in the Laureto Palace, together with his brother, his wife, and later his son.

Theodoric assumed the title of *Dominus*, and later of *Rex*, and—as even Procopius assures us—was a wise and enlightened sovereign. He gave a great impulse to building, undertook extensive work for reclaiming land from the surrounding marshes, and restored Trajan's aqueduct; in fact, some leaden *fistulae* or pipes for the conduct of water found in 1938, bear in relief an inscription which reads: *D(omi)n(us) Rex Theodoricus civitati reddidit*.

Among the great buildings erected by Theodoric his residence, the *Palatium*, must be mentioned and some idea of its exterior appearance—even if only partial—is given by the mosaic showing it at the beginning of the right wall of S. Apollinare Nuovo, but its ground plan is known to us as a result of the excavation carried out by Ghirardini in the early part of this century.

An Arian, and the head of an Arian people, Theodoric wished his subjects to have their own churches. Thus arose the *Anastasis Gothorum*, today the Church of Santo Spirito, which served as a Cathedral, and was near the Arian Baptistery. Beside his Palace Theodoric then erected that stupendous Basilica originally dedicated to the Saviour, today called S. Apollinare Nuovo.

In these churches officiated the Arian Bishops, who, following the teaching of Arius, maintained the heretical doctrine (already condemned by the Council of Nicea in 325 and later by the Council of Constantinople in 381) according to which only God the Father is « *not begotten* », while Christ the Logos is begotten, and he, being different from God, is God by adoption, and not by nature.

In Ravenna there was no violent clash between Arians and Catholics; but some serious conflicts did take place towards the end of Theodoric's reign, for the Sovereign, not satisfied with the results of Pope John's mission (524-525) to the Emperor Justinus in the East and his efforts to obtain favours advantageous to the Arians, kept the Pope a prisoner, and when he died in 526 (little more than three months before Theodoric) he was considered a martyr—*victima Christi*.

In May 540 Belisarius, Justinian's General, succeeded by means of a stratagem in entering Ravenna where the Goths were resisting under the command of Vitiges. Thus the city passed into the hand of the Byzantines, and in 554 became the seat of the Prefecture of Italy. Shortly after, Justinian issued an edict granting to the Catholics all the real estate belonging to the Arians. The baptistery was transformed into the Church of S. Maria, and the Church of the Saviour was « reconciled » and dedicated to St. Martin, the Bishop of Tours who had so strenuously opposed the heretics. The principles of St. Basil held by the Catholic Church were vigorously affirmed, and one can catch an echo as it were, an echo of this reaffirmation in these words written in the book held by Christ in the mosaic that covered the apse of S. Michele in Africisco (now in the Berlin State Museum) which: *Ego et Pater unum sumus* (I and the Father are One).

A few decades later—as a result of the struggles with the Longobards—power passed into the hands of military governors called Exarchs, who may be almost regarded as Viceroys considering that upon them depended, as Andrea Agnello—the 9th century historian, author of the « Liber Pontificalis Ecclesiae Ravennatis »—writes, the *regnum et principatum omnis Italiae* (the kingdom and principality of all Italy). In

Ravenna the Exarchs, who held civil powers as well as military, established a real court of their own, modelled on that of the Emperors.

At first the Byzantines brought back into the city all the pomp and ostentation of oriental life, and beautified their buildings with marbles from Proconnesos and mosaics executed by artists trained perhaps at Byzantium.

Sculpture, which had already in the previous century produced works which, for the wide spacing of the figures, was different both from the iconographic point of view and from that of style, from Italic and Gallic sculpture, now takes on a new aspect; one perceives in parapets and capitals contrasts of light and shade determined by the alternation of mass and space; in panels and altar-fronts, in pulpits and in the « pulvini » surmounting capitals, sculpture now adopts a decorative system which finds its typical mode of expression in scantiness of relief and an increased flatness of modelling.

But this splendid artistic impulse lasted only a short time, partly because the great port of Classe, being no longer the station of the fleet, was neglected and fell into disrepair, and lost its original efficiency, becoming in great part silted up. In fact, Jordanes, who was writing about the middle of the 6th century, tells us that where once the ancient port had been, he saw not masts with sails but trees bearing fine fruit (*quod aliquando portus fuerit, spatiosissimus hortus ostendit arboribus plenus, verum de quibus non pendent vela sed poma*).

In consequence, trade and commerce declined and the city, ill governed for almost two centuries by the Exarchs and then, for a brief period about the middle of the 8th century, by the Longobards and the Franks, was reduced to the end of its strength, and the efforts of the Archbishops to make the Church of Ravenna independent of Rome, were not enough to maintain the dignity and power of the city.

During the epoch of the Ottos, the Archbishops became great feudatories of the Empire, and the city seemed to recover something of its former life.

Thus arose the Comune, among the very earliest in Italy, and with it a *Studio* or University, and a School of Legal Practice (*Ars notaria*). But power soon fell into the hands of the great families, sometimes Guelf, then Ghibelline, who carried on their feud, till, in the 13th and 14th centuries, the Da Polenta family gained the upper hand and became rulers of the city. Among the members of this family we may make special mention of Guido Novello who generously offered hospitality to Dante Alighieri, who had been exiled from Florence and died in Ravenna on September 13th, 1321.

From the beginning of the 15th century Ravenna was under the jurisdiction of the Venetian Republic which exercised direct rule from 1441 to 1509, in which year it passed, by treaty, to the Church. Three years afterwards, the city, defended by the armies of the Holy League, was closely besieged by Louis XII, King of France, who took it by storm with fire and sword (April 12th, 1512).

A long period of obscurity followed, and with the French Revolution Ravenna even lost its rank as Capital of Romagna, an honour which was transferred to Forlì.

After being returned to the Church in 1815, it was the seat of the Legation till 1859, and in the following year it was united to the Kingdom of Italy.

*Coin of Galla Placidia, issued at the time
of Valentinian III*

*Coin of Costanzo III,
husband of Galla Placidia*

This is one of Ravenna's most ancient monuments, and in spite of its small size, one of the most impressive. It is generally believed that it was built by Galla Placidia to serve as her mausoleum, and that the Empress was in fact buried there (Ricci). But historical critics (Gerola and Cecchelli), after a careful examination of ancient sour-

ces, do not share this opinion, not merely because Andrea-Agnello, appealing to tradition, casts doubt on the matter, but above all because it is certain that Galla Placidia died in Rome on November 27th, 450. It is thus much more likely that the Empress was buried in the Rotunda of St. Petronilla adjoining the Basilica of St. Peter in the Vatican which was used as a mausoleum by the family of Theodosius. We know in fact that a few months before her death Galla Placidia had had the body of Theodosius II interred there after having had it brought back from Constantinople.

No ancient source credits Galla Placidia with having erected this little building, yet, considering the fact that it was originally grafted on to the narthex of the neighbouring Church of Santa Croce — a church which was with certainty built by this Empress — it is held that this pious sovereign did indeed order its erection.

The edifice, entirely built in large bricks, is in the form of a cross measuring about 40 ft. by 33 ft., and at the point where the arms cross it is surmounted by a small square tower which protects the semispherical cupola seen in the interior.

Probably it was intended to be a mausoleum, but it must soon have become an oratory — one of the many in which we know Ravenna to have been rich in early Christian times — nor is there any difficulty in believing that it was dedicated to St. Laurence, since the lunette to be seen at the further end of the axis of the chapel contains a figure in mosaic of St. Laurence hastening eagerly towards his coming martyrdom.

Perhaps the notion that the building was the tomb of Galla Placidia is due to the fact that a number of sarcophagi were placed within it, one of them being considered to be that of the Empress. But they were not there originally; the first mention of them goes back only to the early years of the 14th century, to the period when Rinaldo da Concorreggio was Bishop.

The little oratory as it is at present has sunk into the ground about 4½ ft., and this subsidence has considerably modifiied its original aspect, for it now appears to be much too low.

With the exception of the façade, all the sides are adorned with uprights which rest upon a skirting (now below the surface of the ground and so no longer visible) and form arches above, thus breaking the monotony of the wall. The oratory is lit by 14 small windows, the lowest ones having the form of loopholes with embrasures within. In 1908 the window spaces were filled with slabs of alabaster presented by king Victor Emanuel III.

The façade, once covered with marble, was isolated in 1602 when the monks of S. Vitale built the new front of the church of Santa Croce which was placed somewhat further back after the front with its porch was demolished.

If the exterior of the little oratory is very simple and modest, the interior is extremely rich and sumptuous. Indeed it reveals such luxuriance of decoration as veritably to astonish the visitor. An atmosphere dim and subdued, but at the same time, especially on bright sunny days, rendered warm and colourful by the golden light which filters in through the alabaster windows, reigns within the chapel, the upper part of which is completely covered with mosaics, while the lower part has a wide band (almost all restored) of slabs of yellow marble from Siena; the slabs were once of the marble called « giallo antico », as is proved by a few fragments still in their original position.

The wide expanse of the mosaic decoration, which is everywhere very well preserved, has as background for its figures a subdued deep blue colour which often shows modulations in tones of whitish grey, golden and pale blue, together with some sober tints of red, yellow and green. The range of colour is thus so delicately varied and shows such a harmonious accord that we are quite justified today in accepting the judgement given in the 15th century by Ambrogio Traversari who declared he had never seen mosaic so refined and so full of grace (« Musivum nusquam neque tenius, neque elegantius inspeximus »).

The *Lunette* to be seen *on the further wall* shows a personage clad in white bearing on his shoulder a wide cross while his left hand holds an open book upon which we see writing worked in tiny squares separated one from another; evidently is the Hebrew Scriptures. This personage advances towards the centre of the composition where we see a grating with flames beneath it. On the left side is a small cabinet with open doors showing two shelves on which rest four books;

on each of these we read in Latin the name of one of the Evangelists, the books therefore are the four Gospels.

This simple scene has been differently interpreted, for the attempt to identify the personage carrying the book and the cross has given rise to various theories. One theory is that he is a saint hastening to cast a heretical book into flames (A. Venturi). Another (Bottini-Massa) considers the figure in white to be the Angel announcing the Final Judgment. Other have thought he represents Christ coming to judge the living and the dead, and holding a book in which — according to a tradition widely held in the 5th century — are recorded the sins and the merits of men (Filippini). This latter theory has recently been taken up again by Seston, a French scholar, who considers that the flames seen in the middle of the composition are lapping the brass grating mentioned in Exodus XXVII vv. 4-5 as being placed beneath the altar of burnt offering upon which perhaps the sinners were to be immolated. Much more obvious, and therefore more acceptable, is the explanation of those who see in the figure the Roman

martyr *S. Laurence* (De Rossi, Garrucci, Deutschke, Cecchelli, Grabar). In fact, this personage carries the attributes proper to the order of deacons to which St. Laurence belonged i.e. the processional cross and the Book of Psalms, and he has near him what is undoubtedly a gridiron, the instrument of torture proper to him alone. Indeed, considering the determined step with which the saint advances one might conclude that the famous Roman deacon, so much venerated in ancient times, is here shown hurrying towards the fire, or (to use an expression common in ancient stories of the saints) he hastens towards martyrdom — *festinat ad martyrium*.

There is no doubt therefore that the cabinet containing the Gospels appears in the scene as the symbol of the Faith which St. Laurence did not hesitate to give his life.

The mosaic which covers like a soft mantle the barrel vaulting of that arm of the building where this lunette is to be seen, is of highly ornamental character. Upon a dark blue back-ground are many small circles, many stars and many strange flowers. The

Galla Placidia: saved from the wreck (Miniature, 15th century)

same design is to be found on the barrel-vaulting of the other arm lying along the same axis. But here, in the distribution of the various elements of the composition, there is a wider and more restful air. In all ancient Occidental art we find no decorative design resembling this; an ornamentation fairly close to it might be recognised only in a Coptic stuff of the 6th or 7th century in the Egyptian section of the Berlin State Museum, but this stuff was unfortunately destroyed in a fire a few years ago.

The small semispherical *cupola* which marks the point where the four arms of the cruciform building meet, is enlivened by the gleam of more than 800 gold stars which, in ever dimishing circles, surround a *Latin cross* in gold at the top. These stars too shine forth from a dark blue back-ground intended to look like the sky at night. From them seems to emanate a glow which would appear to derive, not so much from the interplay of reflexions, as from the intrinsic nature of the stars themselves.

Lower down, near the four spandrels which support the cupola, stand out all in gold above thin clouds of various hues, the *Symbols of the Evangelists*, the Lion of St. Mark, the Eagle of St. John, the Bull of St. Luke and the Angel of St. Matthew.

It is to be noticed how the Cross that shines has its long arm turned towards the east and not to the main axis of the chapel. This is due to the fact that in ancient times sacred buildings generally had the apse towards the east; but here, as the oratory was grafted on to the narthex of the Church of Santa Croce, the architect was unable to give his building the orientation required by liturgical rule, and the decorator thought that, for his part, he could in intent remedy this by giving the cross in the centre of the starry vaulting the correct orientation.

The high drum supporting the cupola has four *large lunettes* in each of which there is a rectangular window. The mosaicist had to adapt himself to this exigency, and for this reason he placed beside each of the windows two tall male figures. Thus there are eight of them, and each one is wearing a purple-

Mausoleum of Galla Placidia: detail of the decoration

bordered tunic and a cloak adorned with letters. Some are bearded, others not. All, even those of youthful appearance, are in grave and dignified attitudes; with the right arm extended upward they make a gesture of acclamation which Nordström connects with the Cross of the cupola. Above their heads curve wide canopies each in the form of a shell, finished, at the top of the lunette, with a motif of birds' heads and three festoons of pearls.

These personages are no doubt *Apostles*, for one of those on the east side is certainly St. Peter, as is to be concluded from the fact that he grasps in his left hand a key, the attribute exclusively of the Prince of the Apostles. In front of him is St. Paul; this is confirmed by his high bald forehead and pointed beard, for these are the iconographic characteristics of the Apostle of the Gentiles. It is not possible to name the others with certainty, as none has the particular physiognomy which was to distinguish him in later times, nevertheless one must notice that each personage has characteristics that belong to him alone.

The fact that there are only eight Apostles in the lunettes of the drum is due merely to the law of symmetry which is the dominating factor in the decoration of the chapel, and has prevented the artist from placing three figures in each lunette. It would have been a violation of harmony if, in a lunette with a window in the centre, there had been two figures on the right and only one on the left, or vice versa. This is the reason for which the other four Apostles have been in all probability relegated to the barrel-vaulting of the lateral arms in the midst of trailing acanthus.

In their white robes veined with grey and blue, the figures of the Apostles in the lunettes stand out against a back-ground of intense blue, and therefore give almost the impression of being ghosts and apparitions. Only the change in the lower part of the back-ground to a lighter tint, i.e. a yellowish green, seems to give these figures some sort of footing and a certain sense of spacial depth. Among the Apostles below on the grassy field there are little fountains which doves approach or on the edge of which they stand. These are decorative elements which with time took on an allegorical significance, for it is well known that doves are the symbols of souls and that water

alludes to coolness and peace.

The two *lunettes on the east and west sides* have a very similar composition. Here we see two stags which in order to quench their thirst, proceed through a veritable tangle of acanthus branches towards a pool of water surrounded by a ring of grass and flowers. As we gaze at this simple decoration we spontaneously call to mind the verse of the Psalm which undoubtedly inspired the ancient mosaicist: « As the hart panteth after the fountains of water, so my soul panteth after the fountains of water, so my soul panteth after thee, O Good » (Psalm XLII vv. 1-2).

The composition of the *lunette above the entrance* is especially impressive. Amidst a delightful and varied landscape with rocks, trees, grass and bushes, is a pastoral scene against the back-ground of an early morning sky enlivened with light blue tints. In the centre is the figure of the *Good Shepherd* whom the ancient painters had so often frescoed in the Catacombs. But while in the Catacomb painting the Good Shepherd had almost always been represented as a countryman with short tunic and a stick, here he wears a purple mantle covering a tunic of gold and carrying a tall cross in his left hand. In addition a wide gold halo indicating his divinity shines behind his head; a winning expression of serenity and sweetness illuminates his youthful countenance framed by locks of long hair falling on his shoulders.

On either side of him in similar attitudes stand two groups of sheep facing each other. All are looking towards the mystic Shepherd. He is drawn with long curving lines and forms the real pivot of the scene, not only because he is in the very centre of the lunette, but also because, with head turned to one side and right arm to the other, he attracts to himself the main lines of every part of the composition. But what strikes the visitor most as he moves round this little oratory, is that delicate expanse of colours in the mosaic, which, pervading the entire building, leaves him with a feeling of charmed amazement, for the decoration both as regards range of colour and disposition of the subjects represented, blends perfectly with the architecture.

The artists who decorated the oratory — even if we admit theoretically, as some have said, that they came from Africa (Duetschke), or from Constantinople (Strzygowski), or from Syria (Diehl), or from Rome (Kurth and Ricci) — undoubtedly took many elements from the art which after Alexander the Great spread in the near East and in the regions conquered by Rome. Therefore they belong uncontestably to the Hellenistico-Roman school (Muratoff) and it is quite possible that the artists were sent for from Milan after the imperial court had left that city for Ravenna.

At the present time the oratory contains *three marble sarcophagi* which were brought here between the 9th century and the beginning of the 14th. The sarcophagus at the further end, beneath the lunette of St. Laurence, is of truly imposing dimensions. Now it has a somewhat bare and rough appearance because the cornice that adorned the margin and those of the middle panel intended for the inscription have been hacked away. The cover consists of two slabs meeting at a point and has triangular finials at the corners. According to tradition it was the sarcophagus which contained the body of Galla Placidia. In fact, the body — as is stated by various authors from the 14th century to the 16th (for example Rinaldo da Concorreggio and G. P. Ferretti) — could be seen through a large aperture (now closed)

made in the back of the sarcophagus. If this information is correct the body of Galla Placidia must have been placed seated on a chair of cypress wood. Given this extraordinary attitude, there may be some truth in the theory that a body was put inside the sarcophagus, with the intention of passing it off as that of the Empress, in the 13th or 14th century, a period in which the falsification of relics was common, and tales and legends grew up around them (Gerola, Ricci).

In 1577 some boys, overcome by curiosity, thrust some lighted candles through the opening into the tomb, and the light coming in contact with the planks of cypress wood, destroyed everything, save a few fragments of bone, among them a skull, and a few scraps of wood. This was confirmed by Girolamo Rossi in 1577 and by Corrado Ricci in 1899.

Considering the imposing dimensions of the sarcophagus and the lack of any Christian symbol upon it, it is very probable that it is to be regarded as the pagan coffin of some rich and noble personage.

The sarcophagus which is now in the left arm is called the sarcophagus of Constantius III, Galla Placidia's second husband. It was thus called at the beginning of the 14th

Mausoleum of Galla Placidia: sarcophagus of Constantius III

century by Rinaldo da Concorreggio, and this was repeated by Desiderio Spreti in the second half of the 15th century. But Girolamo Rossi, towards the end of the 16th century, mentions a belief that the sarcophagus contained the body of Valentinian III, which is supposed to have been brought from Rome to Ravenna. But all these assertions are without foundation, there is no written record and no earlier evidence to confirm them. In 1738 an investigation was made into the contents of the sarcophagus. The cover was removed — says the eye-witness Fiandrini — and disclosed « two entire heads with a few teeth remaining, and bones covered with soft black mud of about three fingers' breadth in depth ».

On the front of the tomb is a very simple scene. In the centre, upon a rock from which four streams gush out, stands a lamb. Its head is surrounded by a halo inscribed with the monogram of Christ — the Greek letters X and P combined. This proves beyond doubt that we have here the mystic Lamb. At the side of the central figure are two lambs without halos. Probably they stand for Apostles. Two palm trees, one on the right, the other on the left, enclose the composition. This decoration is a motif often used by Christian artists, for the palm — among other things a symbol of victory — recalled verse 13 of Psalm XVI, « Justus ut palma florebit » (The just man shall flourish like a palm tree).

The scene as a whole is well set on the front of the sarcophagus within an elegant cornice. The lambs are realistically drawn, but the rendering of the fleece shows a conventional handling. Stylised elements are also to be noticed in the treatment of the two palms. This sarcophagus may be attributed to about the end of the 5th century. The sarcophagus in the right arm of the oratory is held by some (Rinaldo da Concorreggio), to be of Valentinian III, son of Galla Placidia and Constantius III, and by others (G. Rossi) as that of the Emperor Honorius. But these attributions are also without foundation. In 1738 the bones of two persons, some those of a woman, were to be seen in this sarcophagus.

The front of this coffin, the corners of which are adorned by small fluted columns, has three niches. The lateral ones are exactly alike, and have two spirally fluted columns surmounted by an arch enclosing a shell; below is carved a cross. The shrine in the centre has no arch but a pointed roof; here one sees a tall cross on the lateral arms of which perch two doves. It rests on the rock from which flow the four symbolical rivers, and on it stands the divine Lamb seen in profile with head turned back over the body. The back of the sarcophagus bears a design like that on the front save for some small details, but it is merely sketched.

The cover is of semicylindrical form and the carving represents overlapping scales. It is entirely surrounded by a cornice showing a plait enclosing ovoids. This sarcophagus is to be attributed to the beginning of the 6th century.

THE CATHEDRAL

Of the ancient Cathedral of Ravenna, originally dedicated to the « Aghia Anastasis » i.e. the Resurrection of the Lord, hardly anything remains. The present building (196 ft. long) has a central nave and two aisles and goes back little further than the middle of the 18th century. It was built by the Riminese architect Gian Francesco Buonamici, after he had first, by order of Archbishop Farsetti, demolished the ancient Ursian Basilica with its five naves supported by 56 columns; this building had, however, been considerably altered from time to time during the course of the centuries.

The ancient church — the largest within the walls of Ravenna's civic limits, was built, as the name implies, by Bishop Ursus who must have occupied the episcopal throne, not in the last years of the 4th century, as some scholars think (Bjvanck, Bettini), but during the first decades of the 5th (Testi-Rasponi). It is indeed natural to connect the building of that magnificent edifice with the changed conditions in Ravenna, after the Emperor Honorius had transferred his court thither from Milan, at the beginning of the 5th century, since, at that time, it must have been considered incompatible with the Emperor's residence that the Christian community should continue to meet — as says the first historian Andrea-Agnello — « in huts » i.e. in small oratories or at least in very modest buildings.

The investigations carried out in 1731 made it possible to establish the fact that the earliest level of the church's mosaic pavement (a fragment of which is preserved in the Archiepiscopal Museum) is to be found about 10 ft. below the present one. Moreover at the beginning of this century Gerola was able to ascertain that the apse of the early building (in part preserved beneath the existing apse, but no longer visible) backed on to a part of the wall of the Roman city. The vault of the apse was originally adorned with mosaics, but these must have been destroyed a few centuries later, because in 1112 the entire decoration of the apse was renewed. These new mosaics were destroyed in 1734 by Buonamici, after he himself had made a drawing in order to preserve a record of them. Now only a few fragments remain and these are to be seen in the Archiepiscopal Museum.

Not just before the opening of the 12th century (Ricci), but rather near the end of the 10th (Gerola, Verzone) a spacious crypt was built beneath the choir; it can no longer be visited as it is always full of water. It is of the type which stands between those of semianular form and those that have the form of an oratory. The central part is roofed by cross vaulting having ribs, while it finishes at the end in barrel-vaulting, partly resting on marble columns of varying sizes, surmounted by capitals or « pulvini » each different from the others. It is clear that this material came from other buildings.

The erection of the *Campanile* is assigned to about the same period as the crypt; it is a round bell-tower and is about 115 ft. high. Its original level was more than 6 ft. below the present. As the historian Andrea-Agnello — so scrupulous in giving details relating to the churches of Ravenna — never mentions bell-towers, it has been thought that they were not built till after his time, and that they belong to a period between the 9th century and the 11th. In any case, the oldest historical information at present known concerning the bell-towers of Ravenna is that which refers to the work done in 1038 to the bell-tower of the Cathedral by Archbishop Gebeardo.

With regard to the round form of several of Ravenna's bell-towers, it is held to be derived from that of the towers containing stairways, seen in the city walls e.g. the cylindrical towers, so well known, which flanked the Porta Aurea till the end of the 15th century.

In the *interior* of the Cathedral several works of early Christian and Byzantine sculpture are preserved.

A sarchophagus of about the middle of the 5th century is used as a front for the third altar of the right aisle. Now it contains the bones of the Bishops Esuperantius and Maximian. On its face it shows *Christ between two Apostles*; beyond them are also two palm trees laden with dates.

Of the second half of the 5th century are the two imposing sarcophagi seen in the *Chapel of the Blessed Virgin (Vergine del Sudore)* at the end of the right transept. More ancient is the one in which the body of *Archbishop Rinaldo da Concorreggio* was laid in 1321. The scene carved on the front is so impressive that — as Toesca justly says — it would seem to have derived from some vast mural decoration rather than to

The Cathedral: the mosaic decoration of the 13th century which adorned the apse and the arch of the choir in the ancient Ursian Basilica

The Cathedral: the so-called sarcophagus of Barbatianus

The Cathedral: sarcophagus of Archbishop Rinaldo da Concorreggio

have been conceived for the narrow front of a sarcophagus. Here Christ is seen enthroned and motionless upon the mount from which flow the four symbolical rivers. In his left hand he holds the open book, while with his right he welcomes St. Peter and St. Paul who hasten to him with rapid steps, bearing on their hands covered with their cloaks the signs of martyrdom and victory. This subject, which is well spaced out, is framed at the sides by two stiff palm trees identical even in their crescent -shaped mass of foliage, and above by light clouds. These naturalistic features do not give an effect of landscape, but, with their calculated symmetry and planned rhythmical quality they seem to have their part in this solemn vision. The sarcophagus has a heavy arched lid, of the type also called « a baule » (like a trunk).

The *sarcophagus of St. Barbatianus* is now so called because the bones of Galla Placidia's confessor and advisor were placed within it in 1658. The front is partitioned into niches, and here, for the last time in the early Christian sculpture preserved at Ravenna, we see Christ between S. Peter and St. Paul. The three figures are perfectly frontal, and they are completely independent of one another. Their eyes are fixed on vacancy, the drapery of their garments is formalised, their attitudes rigid. One might almost say that both Christ and the Apostles have assumed the appearance of ghosts. In each of the two lateral niches is a vase with curved handles from which springs a plant resembling a lily just coming into leaf.

Very famous and important for the history of Byzantine sculpture is the marble *pulpit* about half way along the central nave on the right hand. On the two sides runs an inscription which reads: « Servus Xpi Agnellus episc. hunc pyrgum fecit » (The servant of Christ Bishop Agnellus made this pulpit). From it we learn that the sculpture goes back to the time of Archbishop Agnellus (556-569). We have here a characteristic type of pulpit in Greek marble resembling a low tower which is elliptical instead of cylindrical; it is divided into two almost equal parts by means of two openings in which, between sloping parapets, steps were laid. The decoration is the same on both sides: horizontal and vertical friezes crossing at right angles divide the surface into 36 panels set in six horizontal zones. In each panel is carved an animal which varies from zone to zone; working from the top downwards, we see: a lamb, a peacock, a stag, a dove, a duck, and a fish. The idea which inspired it is typically Byzantine, because based on the constant monotonous repetition of the same decorative motifs, which, though they have a symbolic meaning, seem to fade into a merely ornamental repetition. The animals, flat and devoid of plasticity, stand out on a small smooth field within their panel.

Among the works of art of more recent times we may mention the *Chapel of the Blessed Sacrament* at the further end of the left transept. Built in the early 17th century according to the design of Carlo Maderno, it was frescoed by Guido Reni and some of his disciples.

The Cathedral:
the pulpit erected by Bishop Agnellus

The first stone of this church was laid on Sept. 13th, 1553, and the solemn consecration of the edifice took place on Oct. 8th, 1606. The erection of this monumental basilica was due to the Canons Regular of the Lateran, who had about fifty years earlier abandoned their church of S. Maria in Porto which stood outside the city and which Dante mentions as the

.   .   .   . *casa*
Di Nostra Donna in sul lito Adriano
(Paradise, Canto XXI)

(The house of Our Lady on the Adriatic coast). Despite its isolated position almost three miles from the city, it was razed to the ground in an air raid in 1944 resulting in the irremediable destruction of the fine 14th century frescoes with which Pietro da Rimini (Toesca) had adorned the interior.

The great church which the Canons Regular built in the city, partly with material from the church of S. Lorenzo in Caesarea, shows a white façade in Istrian stone divided into two sections. It is majestic and imposing and is adorned with half-columns and various statues, many of which are the work of Cignaroli; it was finished in the last quarter of the 18th century by the architect Camillo Morigia who, with regard to the lower part, adhered to the lines of an earlier design.

The *interior* (223 ft. by 152 ft.) is in Renaissance style showing Palladian taste; it has a vast and solemn air. The nave is separated from the two aisles by pillars alternating with columns, and crowned at the height of the transept by a lofty cupola (158 ft.).

On the High Altar there is a marble bas-relief of the Virgin at prayer; it is known as the « *Greek Madonna* ». This fine figure, which may be of the 11th century (Cecchelli), is of late Byzantine type and was probably brought to Ravenna at the time of the Crusades. According to the legend it flew to the Adriatic shore where it alighted at dawn on April 8th, 1100, preceded by two Angels carrying torches.

Behind the altar is a precious porphyry vase; tradition declares it to be one of the pitchers which, during the marriage feast at Cana, contained the water that the Saviour

S. Maria in Porto: marble relief representing the Virgin

was to change into wine. It is probably a cinerary urn (Delbrueck).

Around the apse we see a fine set of *Choir stalls* in wood; they were carved between 1576 and 1593 by the hand of a French artist, Mastro Marino.

Close by the church of S. Vitale stands the National Museum which is reached from the grassy expanse that lies before the entrance into the church. One enters through a small but elegant portico with Verona red columns. On the lintel of the graceful 16th century doorway are carved the words of Virgil: « Procul o procul este prophani ». The Museum occupies the cloister of the ex-Benedictine monastery, and is due to the amalgamation, carried out by the sculptor Enrico Pazzi, of the collections made by the monks of Classe and those of S. Vitale, with certain modern collections.

In the *first cloister* which in the sober lines of its architecture bears the stamp of fine Renaissance art, the objects are mainly of a funerary character, and were placed here in 1950: some *sarcophagus fronts*, some *sepulchral pillars (stele)* with portraits of the dead persons and various funeral tablets. Many of these, carved on rectangular slabs, belong to the « classiarii » i.e. the soldiers of the Roman fleet stationed in the Port of Classe. Almost all of them were discovered in the 18th century, not far from S. Apollinare in Classe, where, before the church was built, there was a large cemetery. The inscriptions on them are very simple but exceedingly interesting. As a rule they give not only the names of the soldiers and the places whence they came (Egypt, Syria, Dalmatia etc.), but also a record of the ships in which they served, their age and the length of service.

The series of funeral pillars is especially worthy of note. Some of them bear portraits of the dead men, and of the members of their households, including freedmen and slaves. The most famous among them is the one in three storeys made at the beginning of the 1st century A. D. for himself and his family by a certain Publius Longidienus, who was, as the inscription tells us, a ship's carpenter (« faber navalis »). Moreover he wished to be shown on the lower part of the monument in the act of working with an axe on a ship which is being built and which is seen standing upon three high supports.

Very interesting also — especially for the vigour of some of its portraits — is the « stele » in four storeys belonging to the families Firmia and Latronia.

Near the « stele » of Publius Longidienus is the famous sculpture in marble: the *relief with the portraits of members of the Julius-Claudian Family*. Some of the personages still keep the secret of their identity, yet according to the latest studies (M. Santangelo), the individuals, reading from right to left, seem to be as follows: Augustus, Livia, Marcellus, Agrippa, and a seated female deity. It is a fine and accurate piece of work, and translates into relief the contemporary products of the statuary art (Strong).

In a room whose entrance is beside this

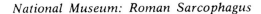

National Museum: Roman Sarcophagus

National Museum: Apotheosis of Augustus

relief all the existing margle remains of the *Porta Aurea* have been placed. This gate in the walls of Ravenna was built in 43 A.D by the Emperor Claudius. Among the fragments the ones most worthy of mention are the two great circular « patere », or discs, adorned with an exterior ring of bead and reel ornament, a wreath of oak leaves and a wide band with palm motifs.

Along the walls of the *second cloister* with its fine columns grouped in pairs — the work of Andrea da Valle, a disciple of Falconetto — we see arranged in chronological order, sculpture fragments of early Christian, Byzantine, Romanesque, Gothic, Renaissance and Baroque art. Among the most interesting pieces may be mentioned the *Sarcophagus of the Traditio Legis* which belongs to the early years of the 5th century (the sculpture shows Christ granting the primacy of his church to St. Peter, to whom he hands the book of the Law); there are also some *capitals* from the demolished church of S. Andrea dei Goti; in one of these, amid large acanthus leaves which seem to be blown out by the wind, is the monogram of the words « Theodericus Rex ».

The *small rooms* which follow one another *on the first floor* of this second cloister contain materials of very different kinds. Noteworthy are some *Greek portraits* (among them Miltiades, Epicurus and Carneades) which were found on various occasions, from 1936, in the Adriatic about five miles out at sea between Porto Corsini and the mouth of the river Reno. They seem to have formed part of a cargo of works of art coming from Rome whence they were sent in the second half of the 16th century by the younger Cardinal Ippolito d'Este to the Duke Alfonso d'Este at Ferrara. They were cast into the sea when the ship in which they were being carried was in danger of sinking, or else they went down with the ship. They were all Roman copies of those ornamental heads which were often used to adorn the villas and libraries of the ancients.

In the *so-called Byzantine room* we note especially four fine « *transenne* » or large open-work panels of the 6th century, three of which certainly came from S. Vitale. The marble is cut rather than sculptured, thus producing a lively colouristic effect resembling black and white. Thanks to the great skill of those who executed the trepanning, the marble surface comes to resemble embroidery with fantastic designs of stylised leaves, branches and coils which take on a rigid appearance as if they had undergone a process of cristallization. The symbolic motifs grafted on to these intricate patterns — such as peacocks, crosses and doves — seem almost to lay aside their religious significance, in order the better to attain an

The National Museum: ceramic plate of the factory of Castelli with a scene of a triumph

exquisitely pictorial and supremely decorative effect.

Another celebrated work of sculpture in this room — which also contains the original *bronze cross* that surmounted the roof of S. Vitale till 1911 — is the great bas-relief representing the third of the twelve labours of Hercules: *the capture of the Deer* (here it is clearly a stag). The relief, which goes back perhaps to the end of the 5th century, is of particular importance, because, if the scheme is inspired by the models of Greek art of the 4th century B.C., the rendering reveals the essential spirit of Byzantine art: to transform plasticity into pictorial sculpture.

The same intention is seen in the fine open-work *capital* — a work not much earlier than the middle of the 6th century — which came from the destroyed church of S. Michele in Africisco.

Very important too are the *circular window-panels* of various brilliant colours. They are from the windows of the apse of S. Vitale, and must be considered the most ancient specimens of window-glass belonging to a church (Cecchelli).

The *collection of stuffs* from Coptic to Renaissance specimens, boasts two pieces that are very famous, both being assigned to the 9th century. The first is the so-called « Velo di Classe »; it consists of three lengths embroidered with various busts of Veronese Bishops. Originally intended for the altar of the relics of the Saints Fermo and Rustico at Verona, it was eventually brought to the Ravennate monastery at Classe. The second piece comes from the tomb of S. Giuliano at Rimini: it is fine silk material, now brown in colour, with two rows of small circles; in the centre of each of these a lion seems lightly and watchfully to advance; the form of these animals and of the other decorative motifs which adorn the stuff recalls the art of the Sassanid dynasty of Persian Kings.

The *collection of ivories* is one of the most precious sections of the Museum, there are specimens of remote and of recent times. The most ancient, perhaps of the 5th century or the early 6th, is the one showing *Apollo with his cithern and Daphne*. It is not impossible, considering the subject, that it was the cover of one of those containers mentioned by the grammarian Papia, intend-

ed to the *cover for the Evangelistary* which origin (Volbach). The same origin is attributed to che *cover for the Evangelistary* which was brought from the Camaldolese monastery of S. Michele at Murano to the one at Classe. It consists of five parts, and is sometimes referred to as « the five-sided cover of Murano ». It bears a representation of Christ enthroned above the scene of the three young Hebrews in the furnace. Around we see four of the miracles of Jesus, and underneath, two episodes from the story of Jonah.

The *collection of ceramics* also comprises precious treasures, for there are products of the most celebrated factories, from those of Deruta to those of Faenza, from those of Urbino to those of Castelli. The most noted of all are two large plates in metallic lustre ware; they are of Hispano-Moorish workmanship belonging to the last quarter of the 15th century, and are decorated with a series of small leaves arranged in concentric circles. One has a ram in the centre, and the other the sign of Capricorn.

There is a very original cup from Faenza belonging to the 15th century; it was found in 1914 in the excavation of St. Agatha. Its enamel is of exquisite workmanship and it retains an uncommon transparency of colour. It is a loving cup bearing the figure of a woman holding a book in her right hand, and in her left a cup containing two eyes. Near the outer edge runs the Latin inscription beginning: « Faciat unusquisque quod vult sive... » (Let each do as he will or... ». Around the bottom we read an inscription which consists of a combination of letters and musical notes in the usual four clefs in key F. It is a love song which ends with the lament: « Tu solla sei che mi fai languire cum la mia faretra che mi passato il core sol fa mio possente amore già non posso abandonare » (Thou alone art she who makes me languish with my quiver, who hast pierced my heart so that I cannot now abandon my great love).

The Museum possesses also a rich *collection of Creto-Venetian icons* of the periodo from the 14th century to the 18th, and a valuable *numismatic section* containing more than 6600 specimens. Among them are some gold coins of Galla Placidia and Justinian, and also some medals by Pisanello and Benvenuto Cellini.

The National Museum: The Roman funeral stele of Publius Longidienus

The Curch of S. Vitale has always awakened the liveliest admiration. Indeed, while in the first half of the 9th century Andrea-Agnello wrote that no building in Italy could be compared with S. Vitale as regards the form and plan of the edifice, Choisy, the well known historian, could declare, during the last century, that never had stability, originality, splendour of colour and purity of line—the genious of Rome and that of the East—been associated in such a fascinating and harmonious whole.

The Church was begun by Bishop Ecclesius after his return from his mission to Byzantium in 525 together with Pope John. For this reason it is considered that the building was commenced in the reign of Amalasuntha, ·who succeeded her father Theodoric in 526, and adopted a policy of wider toleration towards the Catholics.

Reliable historical information tells us that the funds required for building (it cost 26000 « soldi » of gold) were put at the disposal of the Bishop by Julianus Argentarius; we do not know exactly who this influential personage was. It has been said that he was the architect of the building (Rivoira, Lugli) and also the treasurer of the Church in Ravenna (Von Quast, Ricci), but these theories have now been rejected, and it seems more likely that he was a wealthy private banker (Hartmann, Rosenberg, Schubart and Deichmann), though we need entirely exclude the idea that may have been at the same time a sort of « longa manus » of Justinian (Testi-Rasponi, Von Simson), that is, one ordered by the Emperor to act in Ravenna as a kind of fifth column, with the duty of preparing the ground, thus facilitating the conquest of the city by the Byzantines, who occupied it in the year 540.

The Church, though begun by the Goths, was finished under the Byzantines, for it was consecrated in May 547, if not, as is perhaps more likely, in 548 (Testi-Rasponi), but its founder, Bishop Ecclesius, did not live to see the completion of the building, nor did his immediate successors, the Bishops Ursicinus and Victor, since we know that the solemn consecration of the church took place during the episcopate of Maximian, the great ruler born at Pola who was the first in Ravenna to assume the title of Archbishop.

The edifice, which has an octagonal plan, is built with the typical bricks somewhat long and thin, which were used only in the buildings erected by Julianus Argentarius. The exterior reveals the way in which the space within is divided, for the upper and narrower part, covered with a pyramidal roof, hides and protects the cupola, while the lower and wider part allows for two ambulatories or arcades around the walls, one upon the ground floor and the other, the *matroneum*, above it.

The rhythmic regularity of line imparted by the octagonal plan is even more conspicuous in the apse as a whole, for it is flanked by the *prothesis* and *diaconicon* (the two small chapels typical of Byzantine sacred edifices) which, with their varied play of volume, throw into relief the emphasis on height shown by the architectural forms on this side.

Almost opposite the apse is the *narthex*, or ancient entrance to the church. The form is that of a porch with semicircular side walls, facing each other in a way suggesting a pair of pincers. In front of it there was originally an atrium, of which Maioli found with the main axis of the church, for it does not stand against the side of octagon which faces the apse, but is on one of the angles. It is therefore linked with the two sides which meet at that point by the two triangular spaces which result, and at the wide end of these rise the two round towers in which were the stairways leading to the matroneum in ancient times.

This curious position of the porch with regards to the building has been explained in various ways. Some scholars have thought that it was due to the presence on the site of some small chapels for which—despite their destruction because of their being within the area of the new building—a respectful memory was necessary (Ricci, Gerola). Others have upheld that the expedient was determined by the desire to give the entrance a more imposing appearance, and at the same time to find a solution of the problem which would enable the towers to be more closely united with the main building (Jackson). Moreover there has not been lacking some who think that this unsymmetrical arrangement was due solely to artistic or structural reasons (Jonescu). Others—perhaps with closer adherence to reality—have found the explantation in the opportunity gained of making two doorways on two sides of the octagon, instead of the single opening afforded by one side (Toesca).

The *interior* of the church is the more impressive because, though the shadow is deepest and lingers more in the two colonnades along the walls, the central space is flooded with light. This contrast gives rise to a strange pictorial effect which is greatly increased by the alternation of space and mass afforded by the eight tall massive pillars that support the cupola, and alternate with the wide window spaces that seem intended to make the architectural structure as little material as possible.

Particular mention must be made of the great cupola, not, certainly, for the late 18th century frescoes, which, not to mention other defects, give a wrong impression of the structure—but rather for the system with which it was carried out. The architect, in fact, not only achieved his object by making use of the usual light material consisting of terracotta tubes inserted one within the other and placed horizontally in double rows to form circles growing smaller and smaller as one row placed upon another, but also by striving to diminish the lateral pressure as much as possible. To this end he considered it best to make the weight of the great cover fall as far as possible on the eight massive pillars below, by giving the cupola a conical outline that tended to get the pressure of the whole exercised rather in a vertical direction.

According to some scholars the architecture of S. Vitale is the last expression in the West of the constructive methods and spacial forms typical of Roman art (Rivoira, Bet-

S. Vitale: detail of the mosaic of the apse

tini); others, on the contrary, think that it represents one of the most characteristic examples of Byzantine architectural genius (Strzygowski, Diehl).

In our modest opinion a compromise is possible between these two contrasting theories, not because this is one of the simplest ways of solving the problem, but because it answers effectively to concrete and positive facts. We must remember that Bishop Ecclesius began building the church on his return from the East where he must have been impressed by more than one of the churches with central plan, and such churches were rather rare in the West. By this, we do not intend to deny that oriental building with concentric plan derived in their turn from western systems of building, but in them some features genuinely their own were undoubtedly elaborated. It is therefore our personal opinion that, both as regards plan as well as structure, S. Vitale is, after all, a Roman building; but the fount of inspiration is not to be found in Italy, but rather in eastern regions.

Moreover, one should remember the circumstance that in S. Vitale certain architectural features typically Byzantine are to be found, such as the « pulvini » and capitals, the latter of which show open-work, in that the surface carving has been cut away and isolated from the stone behind, thus producing the appearance of a light embroidery rich in geometrical motifs and plant designs. ,

The *mosaic decoration* is all concentrated in the deep well-lit choir and apse. We have here an artistic complex of the highest order, due to the activity of two different artistic schools. The work in the choir is that of a school trained in the Hellenistico-Roman tradition; the mosaicists of the apse were of pure Byzantine education. We can be sure of this by noting the principal differences; in the mosaics of the choir the personages are figured, in the most varied positions, some are seen in frontal attitude, some in profile, some half way between the two; some are standing; others are seated, some are bending down, others standing erect, some are resting, others are in movement. In the mosaics of the apse, on the other hand, all the personages—excepting only the Christ in the centre of the cupola—are always shown in frontal position, always standing upright, always stiff and motionless.

Beneath the clothing of the figures in the choir we can often catch a glimpse of the anatomical structure of the body, we often note the form of the limbs. Nothing of this can be seen in the figures in the mosaics in the apse; on the contrary, the garments seem to fall rigidly like cloaks of metal. Again, in the choir the personages stand out against a lively landscape with rocks, trees and clouds. In other words the scene is drawn direct from nature. But behind the figures of the apse we see only an unbroken expanse of gold which offers no sylvan landscape, but rather seems to lift the scene to a trascendental plane which might be said to lie beyond time and space.

But these undeniable differences do not imply that it is necessary to assign the two groups of mosaics to different epochs. One might rather say that they were executed about the same time, those of the choir being perhaps a little earlier than those of the apse.

The truth is, that in the same period, artists were living who followed quite different ideals. There was—as there is today—a crossing and interweaving of various currents. As a result, we may say that in S. Vitale the decoration of the apse was entrusted to workers who found their pictorial ideal in an artistic world quite different from that which inspired the mosaicists who planned the ornamentation of the walls and vaulting of the choir.

The *Choir*. Access is marked by a great arch on the intrados of which on a dark background there are fifteen medaillons which start from the summit where the figure of the *Redeemer* is seen, and contain gold haloed busts of the *Twelve Apostles* and two others, presumed to be the sons of S. Vitalis, the *Saint Gervasius* and *Protasius*. Each medaillon is separated from the next by two dolphins with tails crossed, and is surrounded by a series of lively luminous motifs showing globes and crosses.

The decoration on the left wall is, like that on the right, marked by great naturalism; moreover, there is a strict correspondence between the two walls as regards the plan of the composition.

On the left side, above the great « trifora » (or two-pillared opening into the lower ambulatory) the space is filled by a large lunette in which we see *two episodes in the life of Abraham;* first, the Patriarch is seen offering hospitality to the three

Angels who announce to him and his wife Sarah, seen standing on the threshold of the hut, the birth of a son, and then the sacrifice of that son, Isaac, by Abraham who hastens thus to obey God's will. Not only are the two scenes wonderfully adapted to the curve of the lunette, they are also noteworthy for certain details in the treatment of the figures. Above all it is interesting to observe the masterly manner and fine taste with which the artist has avoided the usual uniformity in the position of the three seated Angels by slightly inclining the heads of the lateral ones, and above all in the varied positions of their hands and feet. Beautiful too is the group showing Abraham about to complete the sacrifice, because of its pyramidal scheme which has at the summit the drawn sword of the Patriarch, and at the extremities of the base, the altar upon which is the half-kneeling figure of little Isaac, and the ram which after the testing of Abraham, is to take the place of the human victim.

Above the arch of the lunette are *two Angels in flight* who hold a disc enclosing a cross. On the left side we see the *Prophet Jeremiah*, a large scroll in his hands, while on the right, low down, are the representatives of the *twelve tribes of Israel* grouped round Aaron, and higher up, *Moses* in the act of ascending the rocky slopes of Mt. Sinai to receive the Law from the hand of God which reaches out from a long bank of clouds.

In the upper zone, beside the fine « trifora » with its two magnificent alabaster columns surmounted by beautifully carved capitals, we see two of the Evangelists— *St. John and St. Luke*— who are depicted in the midst of a naturalistic scene not wanting in stylised elements, awaiting inspiration to write their Gospels; this is the reason why a short of small table with pens and inkstand is seen beside them. They are grave and solemn personages who wear purple-bordered tunics and white mantles, while at their feet, ducks and other aquatic birds swim on limpid waters. Above the heads of the two Evangelists appear their respective symbols: the Eagle and the Bull.

Above the arch of the « trifora » on the outer side there is a decoration of vine branches which spring from two large vases and unfold in a series of volutes or coils. A similar decoration is seen above the arches of the upper « trifora » on the opposite wall,

and a composition—exactly corresponding to the one mentioned above—is seen in the lateral zones in which the Evangelist appear —*St. Matthew and St. Mark*—shown in about the same position as the other two. Above them are their symbols: the Angel and the Lion, and below them again are aquatic creatures, among the most charming of which are a heron and a tortoise.

The great lunette above the *lower* « trifora » is surmonted by the usual design of *two Angels in flight*. On their right is the *Prophet Isaia*, and on the left, down below, we see *Moses watching the flocks of his father-in-law*, and above *Moses unfastening his sandals to approach the burning Bush*, which is shown by bright tongues of flame arising from a rocky ground.

Within the lunette—as in the one in front —two scenes are shown; they are the *Sacrifice of Abel and that of Melchizedek*. The two men advance, the one from the left the other from the right, towards an altar raised on four small columns and completely covered with an embroidered cloth. Abel, who stands near a poor hut and a tree edged along the trunk and the leafy top with a gleam of white, is clad in a short skin and a bright red cloak; he carries a lamb in his arms, Melchizedek, behind whom stands a sumptuos temple, wears rich garments reaching to his feet; he advances with a loaf of bread, and is looking upwards to the point where the hand of God appears among the clouds.

It has justly been observed that the composition in this lunette, though airy and not without organic structure, is perhaps to be considered somewhat inferior to the opposite one showing scenes in the life of Abraham (Toesca). But in any case the subjects in both are well suited to the place they occupy, for, being at the sides of the altar, they seem artistically to join in the beautiful prayer which, both in ancient days and in our own, is repeated by the priest at Mass after the Consecration: « Above them (the bread and the wine) do Thou vouchsafe to look with favourable and gracious countenance and accept them, as Thou didst vouchsafe to accept the gifts of Thy just servant Abel, and the sacrifice of our Patriarch Abraham, and that which Thy High Priest Melchizedek offered unto Thee, a holy Sacrifice, an unspotted Victim ».

The choir has a ribbed cross-vaulting bearing a luxurious decoration which covers

S. Vitale: The mosaic decoration of the Presbytery 31

it so completely that one might say the artist must have had a real horror of empty spaces—*horror vacui*. Along the ascending lines of the triangles rise four bands adorned with leaves and fruit meeting at the summit in a wreath which encloses the white figure of the *Lamb of God* (*Agnus Dei*) standing out against a sky lit up by a myriad of stars. Towards this central medaillon also converge the out-stretched arms of four Angels who stand upon azure globes and set in the midst of a green expanse of acanthus branches, whose coils are brightened with gold and give the impression of being as it were lightly touched by continual vibrations of air and light.

Here in the choir the whole decoration is inspired by nature, and the colour lends its powerful aid to impart vigour and freshness to the various figures.

More tense is the colour of the mosaics of the choir arch where there is an unbroken background of gold against which we see the two *Angels*, flying in a horizontal position and holding up a disc crossed by eight rays of light which come from a central Alpha. At the sides of these angels are two green cypress trees, and then a representation of the *City of Jerusalem and the City of Bethlehem* with walls studded with gems and precious stones; they are symbols respectively of the Church of the Jews and the Church of the Gentiles.

It is a truly divine vision that we see in the dome of the apse. On a field dotted with flowers and varied by two layers of rocks lying one upon the other, while four symbolical rivers gush forth from the centre, stand five personages. In the centre is the *Redeemer*, young and beardless, seated upon a globe of vivid blue. Beside him stand *two Archangels*. He is clad entirely in purple and his halo is signed with a cross. In his left hand he holds the scroll with the seven seals, and with his right he offers the triumphal crown to *St. Vitalis* who advances from the left ready to receive it with hands covered by his mantle. From the opposite side comes *Bishop Ecclesius*, carrying a model of the church he had begun, the form of which is that which the church actually has.

All these figures are of the same height and are set against a gold back-ground which is enlivened above by the presence of thin whitish blue and whitish pink clouds, and these, relieving the radiant splendour of the wide surface with its metallic glow, by introducing a naturalistic touch, may be due to the suggestion of a local artist.

As the vault of the apse displays the court of Heaven, so, lower down in the two sections at the side, we see the earthly court with all the pomp and ostentation of the East.

In the left one is seeing the *Emperor Justinian* who carries a gold paten in his hands. Preceded by a subdeacon swinging a censer, a deacon carrying the Book of the Gospels, and Bishop Maximian—the only person to have his name written above his head—the Emperor is seen accompanied by three high dignitaries and is followed by soldiers of the guard.

All these persons are shown full-face, stiff and static, their figures, without solidity of form, seem to have become incorporeal, fixed in simple rhythmic expressions. One has almost the feeling that the slow procession has made a right about face, but only in order to let itself be admired for a few minutes, the pause will be brief, the slow advance may be resumed at any moment.

The colour in the garments of these personages is widely spread, especially as regards to white and the purple. Yet a heightening of tone by means of brilliant colours is not lacking, it is provided by the bright tints—greens and reds—of the soldiers' garment. In this panel the figures which most attract attention are those of Justinian and Maximian; the former, with diadem and nimbus, represents the temporal power (« regalis potestas »), the second, with pallium and cross, the attributes of episcopal rank, stands for the spiritual power (« sacrata auctoritas »).

The countenance of Justinian must certainly have been drawn according to the fixed conventions for imperial portraits that were sent out into the provinces, but that of Maximian was certainly delineated by an artist who knew the real features of the Bishop; so this emaciated face, with its clearly marked characteristics and enlivened by penetrating blue eyes may be taken to be the finest portrait among all those preserved in the mosaics of Ravenna. Looking again at the Bioshop's slender figure, the head with its scanty locks of hair, and the face lit up by the blue eyes—which caused a famous Italian painter (Severini) to compare it with one of Cezanne's self-portraits—one

S. Vitale: Throne of Neptune (detail)

recalls the words with which the first historian, Andrea-Agnello, described the saintly Bishop: « He was of tall stature, thin in face, baldheaded save for a few locks of hair, with grey-blue eyes, and adorned with every grace ».

Among the other persons who appear in the panel, and who may be said simply to form the imperial retinue, there is one who seems to have a certain importance; he is the one, with features so typically original as certainly to be taken from life, who is seen between the Emperor and the Bishop in the second plane. We do not know precisely who he was; some critics have suggested that he is Julianus Argentarius (Testi-Rasponi, Von Simson, Rodenwaldt), but recently this supposition has been doubted as improbable, and the latest theory—taking into consideration also the particular position this personage occupies in the picture—is that here we see the « Praetorius » of Italy, the high functionary who represented the imperial authority at the consecration of the church (Deichmann).

The picture on the right, facing the one with the figure of Justinian, represents the *Empress Theodora*, who advances with a golden chalice studded with gems in her hands. She is preceded by two civil dignitaries and is followed by a crowd of court ladies. She seems about to leave the throne room of her palace rather than to be on the point of entering the church (Visser, Cecchelli).

In this panel, as in the other, the wide expanses of white and purple are again used, but here too the colour becomes vivid and brilliant, as can be seen in the glowing silk robes of the ladies, which, by the brightness of their colours seem to catch the leitmotiv of that blue, white and red curtain hanging above.

Theodora, adorned with a rich diadem set with pearls and gems, is wrapped in an ample purple mantle the lower part of which is embroidered in gold with the scene of the Wise Men bringing their gifts to the Holy Child. There is no doubt that the artist, by introducing this scene into the Empress's robe, wished to suggest an obvious comparison, wished in fact to express this idea: « As the Wise Men bring gifts to the Child Jesus, so we, Justinian and Theodora, offer our gifts to Christ » (Grabar). Thus it is clear that the scenes in the two panels are not so much—as Tea has said— a representation of the offering which in ancient times the faithful used to make after the reading of the Gospel, as a representation of the « oblatio Augusti et Augustae » i.e. that gift of liturgical vessels which the Byzantine Emperors often made to the most important churches in the territories over which they ruled.

While in the panel showing Justinian there are two conspicuous persons, as we have seen, in the panel showing Theodora there is only one who dominates the scene; it is the Empress herself, who is taller than the other ladies.

Since it has been noticed that only the

33

first two ladies who follow Theodora have expressive faces, while the others all have the same stereotyped look, an attempt has been made to name these two ladies. A not improbable theory identifies them as Antonina and Giovannina, wife and daughter of Belisarius who had conquered Ravenna; this is all the more likely as we learn from the historian Procopius of Caesarea, that they were the Empress's intimate friends.

It is to be noted how all the figures, by now devoid of any material reality, have no value here save that of rhythm of line and the repeated cadences of a musical composition, and how the colour reaches its highest brilliance in the display of enamel and mother-of-pearl which, by the small size of the « tesserae » and their varied arrangement, give rise to a striking interplay of a thousand lights and a thousand reflexions.

On the side walls of the choir, very close to the great arch that gives access to it, are inserted two marble fragments that formed part of the so-called « Throne of Neptune »,

a sculpture of the Hellenistico-Roman age. They show cherubs bearing the attributes of some divinities against an architectural background.

In the circular chapel to the right of the apse a few interesting objects have been preserved: a small *casket* of the 6th century bearing the name of Julianus Argentarius; the broken *sarcophagus of Bishop Ecclesius*, its front adorned with a flat relief showing a cross flanked by two stags, two peacocks and two palms; and a *sarcophagus* of the second half of the 5th century, which, shortly before the middle of the 7th, was used again, to receive the remains (so says the Greek inscription carved on the rounded lid) of the *Exarch Isaccius*. Upon the smooth background of the front of this sarcophagus a few figures in somewhat high relief are roughly carved: they are Wise Men in typical oriental costume—breeches and short tunics with Phrygian caps on their heads— bringing their gifts to the Child Jesus who is seated on the Madonna's lap.

Erected by Archbishop Ursus at the beginning of the V century and adjoining the cathedral, this baptistry like the one adjoining the cathedral in Milan goes back to the IV century, and is also octagonal. Its original level is about nine feet below street level. Originally each of the four flat sides, alternating with four apses, contained a door. To-day only the archway above each is visible.

In the beginning of the second half of the V century Archbishop Neone built a dome over the building and, as the historian A. Agnello, testifies, covered it with magnificent mosaics, still existing today. If the outside of the baptistry shows, on the upper parts pensil arches — and this structure shows clearly a later rebuilding — the inside shows a well calculated series of vertical shiny multicoloured marble marquetries, stuccoes and mosaics, so that architecture and decoration become a single harmonious unit.

The domed roof, constructed with small terracotta tubes to save weight, is completely covered with mosaic decoration which can be divided into three zones, viz: the centre and two concentric zones. In the circle at the very centre of the dome is the Baptism of Christ. Here Christ is shown standing in the waters of the Jordan while St. John goes through the baptist rites and a symbolic personification of the river itself (an old man) emerges to offer the Saviour a green garment to dry Him, (the dove, Christ's head and the right arm of St. John are 18th centuri restorations).

In the second zone (from centre) on an indigo background and separated by thin floral stanchions in golden mosaic, are the twelve apostles in two formations led respectively by St. Peter and St. Paul. The apostles are shown walking slowly, holding symbolic jewelled crowns in their covered hands. The apostles may be identified by the name written by the side of each head. The outside ring contains eight architectural sections, each curving into an apse at the centre: in each of these there is a throne and an altar, alternately, alluding to the majesty and divinity of Christ. The thrones are between two « viridaria » symbol of the celestial gardens, surrounded by transennae; the trees are flanked by two empty seats; alluding to those prepared by Christ, for the Elect. Next a little lower at the height of the windows, are the stucco decorations and figures of the prophets in niches. These motifs, like the mosaics, are of the same period, as Archbishop Neone, (451-475 A. D.). Lower still, within a ring or circle there is a mosaic (much restored) among green acanthus sprays sparkling with gold on the dark blue background. By observing the domed roof as a whole, one sees how the general idea is of a great spoked wheel, rotating around a fixed central nucleus, represented in this case by the centre « medaillon ». Because of the tremendous centrifugal force caused by this effect the decorations suggest the idea of the continuous and infinite.

Cathedral Baptistry:
Marble roman vase

With this church, probably the first church built by Theodoric after his conquest of Ravenna in 493 A.D., the king wanted to give his people, who were Arian, a church distinct from the Catholics, and dedicated it to the Resurrection. In 561 A.D. once the Goths had been driven from the city, the church was consecrated to S. Teodoro the martyr of Amasea, and reconciled to the Catholic cult.

Only later was it re-named, the Spirito Santo. Apart from the difference between the actual and original height of the flooring and columns (1 m. 82 cm.), the interior of the church, which is very luminous, can be said to preserve its original architectural features.

It is divided by two lines of seven columns each, into three naves, and being 26 m. 41 cm. long and 16 m. 99 cm. wide, has thus only limited depth. Under this aspect it brings to mind the proportions of another Arian church, in Rome (built 25 years before): S. Andrea dei Goti. The marble ambo about half way along the pillars on the right is of the Theodoric period.

The lacunar ceiling of the centre nave hiding the former trusses was constructed before the end of the first half of the XVI century, and is of the same period as the small archway in front of the facade. At the bottom of the right hand nave is a large canvas of the Forlivese painter Livio Agresti, showing « Dove Bishops » so called because their election was thought to be due to the appearance of the Dove representing the Holy Ghost.

Just by the ex-Arian Cathedral is the baptistry, now sunken about 2 m 25 cm. into the ground. This is the baptistry that Theodoric built about the end of the V century A.D.

Like the Catholic baptistry this too is octagonal in shape, and has four small apses on alternating walls. Originally the construction was surrounded on seven sides by an ambulatory. The actual protective railing shows part of the perimeter. About 750 A.

D., the Emperor Justinian gave the Arian churches to the Catholics so this baptistry ceased to be used as such and was therefore transformed into a church, « S. Maria in Cosmedin ». The mosaics on the brick domed ceiling are a simplified version of the Catholic Baptistry, since the central medaillon here is surrounded by one concentric strip not two.

The central medaillon shows the Baptism of Christ. Here Christ is shown half immersed in the waters of the Jordan, and with John's right hand placed upon his head in the act of baptising. The river Jordan is symbolized by the austere old man sitting near a vase from which the river springs. This figure is characterized by two divine aquatic attributes: a green rush in his hand, and two red lobster claws above his head.

The encircling ring around this scene shows the twelve apostles two by two, led by St. Peter and St. Paul going towards a throne surmonted by a cross, this being the symbol of Christ's sovereignty). Each apostle, separated from the other by a palmtree, carries jewelled crowns in his veiled hands, except St. Peter who carries the keys, and St. Paul a rolled manuscript. All this has a background of gold.

This mosaic shows two clear styles. The first, including the central medaillon, the throne and St. Peter, St. Paul and the apostle behind the latter, shows a major vigour. The second includes the remaining nine apostles and though only a little later, it has more diffused and paler chromatic tones.

Arian Baptistry

S. Francesco

The church of S. Francesco rises at the far end of a quiet square, bordered on its southern side by the Provincial Administration Offices and on the north by XVI century porches (formerly belonging to the monastery of Porto) and put here in 1936.

The church was built during the last half of the V century by Bishop Neone and was dedicated to St. Peter and St. Paul.

Nothing remains today of this construction, as the whole church was rebuilt in the X and XI centuries. A little earlier than this, the rectangular bell-tower with two, three and four mullioned windows was added. Entrusted to the Franciscan monks in 1261, it was given the name of S. Francesco; and it is here that in 1321 the funeral of Dante was held, whose body (as Boccaccio writes) was encased in a « stone chest » and placed in the portico, which was destroyed some centuries ago.

The inside of the church is divided into three aisles with two rows of antique marble columns and covered by a medieval wooden ceiling representing the reversed keel of a ship. It is striking for its simplicity and harmony of line and draws the visitors' eye to the apse under which a raised presbytery covers the crypt and oratory, built a little before the year 1000 A.D. and visible through small openings. The crypt is constantly under water. The pavement of the crypt is that of the original V century construction with its mosaics, and one can see the Latin inscription referring to the burial of the founder, Archbishop Neone.

Two really beautiful antique marble sarcophagi considered by some to be about the last half of the IV century or the first half of the V, are conserved inside the church. One, partly restored, supports the high altar, the other is to be found about half way along the left hand aisle.

Both of these belong to the type called « a colonne » because their side niches are divided by columns, between which there are figures of Christ and the Apostles.

S. Francesco: Sarcophagus with Christ and the Apostles

In spite of some alterations brought about during the course of the centuries, and in spite of the severe damage caused by an air raid in 1944, this church on the whole retains its original architectural appearance. The atrium which was once in front of it no longer exists, but a lofty mediaeval porch projects in a striking manner adorning the brick façade, while beside it stands the massive square *Campanile* (139 ft. high) from the summit of which issues the sad, mournful sound, as a pious legend says, of the two bells cast in 1208 by a certain Robertus de Sasono.

The sacred building was begun by the Empress Galla Placidia in fulfilment of a vow she made during the dangerous voyage from Constantinople to Ravenna in order to assume the government of the Western Empire for her young son Valentinian III.

Shortly after its erection the church was enlarged so as to take in the space originally intended for the narthex. One can notice signs of this in the double arch to be seen along the side walls as soon as one has crossed the threshold.

The *interior* (163 ft. by 73 ft.) is wide and well lighted and is divided into a central nave and two aisles by two rows of columns which have been raised about 5 ft. above the level of the original flooring.

The choir arch and the semidome of the apse are now covered with simple white plaster, but from the 5th to the 16th century they shone with mosaics of the greatest interest—for they comprised portraits of almost all the members of the family of Theodosius, and twice over a representation of the scene of how St. John the Evangelist saved from destruction the ship in which Galla Placidia was sailing with her children.

The apse, which is semicircular on the inside and polygonal on the outside, is not only, as is usually the case, flanked by the two typical rectangular chapels known as the « diaconicon » and the « prothesis », but shows an unusual feature in that continuous series of seven openings, which, supported by elegant marble columns, has the appearance of a loggia. Below this can be seen the outlines of three windows that are now closed. According to some scholars (Ricci, Gerola, Rivoira, Giovannoni) these three windows were closed while the work was still in progress, because of a sudden change in the original plan; according to others (Bettini), the three lower windows and the seven windows higher up, were of the 5th century—with the difference that the former were originally intended to give light, while the others were blind and merely had a decorative value for the exterior. Others again have rejected these theories and have thought that the loggia was opened only on the exterior considerably later, in the 8th century (Galassi) or during the 11th or 12th (Cecchelli).

The fragments of mosaic arranged along the walls came from the various floorings which at different levels (and therefore in various periods) adorned the church. Together with some sections of mosaic belonging to the most ancient floorings, are to be seen various panels of mosaic made in 1213 by order of the Abbot Guglielmo; they show simple popular subjects, fantastic animals, a fox's funeral, and episodes seeming to refer to the Fourth Crusade, as one concludes from representations of the taking of Zara and of Constantinople.

In the chapel opening about half way along the left aisle are the remains of some 14th century frescoes. Those on the vaulting show the *Four Evangelists*, each with his symbol, and the *Doctors of the Church*: St. Jerome, St. Ambrose, St. Augustine and St. Gregory. Some critics have attributed them to Giotto (Ricci), others with greater probability, to Giovanni Baronzio da Rimini (L. Venturi).

S. Giovanni Evangelista: Interior

S. Apollinare Nuovo

The Basilica now called by the name of S. Apollinare Nuovo was originally an Arian church. It was built by Theodoric who dedicated it to the Redeemer. This is definitely stated by a passage in the « Liber Pontificalis Ecclesiae Ravennatis », in which the historian Andrea-Agnello, quoted the inscription which ran upon a band above the windows of the apse: « Theodericus Rex hanc ecclesiam a fundamentis in nomine Domini Domini nostri Jesu Christi fecit » (King Theodoric built this church from its foundations in the name of Our Lord Jesus Christ).

There is thus no doubt that the building of the Basilica must be assigned to the period between 493 when the Goths entered Ravenna, and 526 when Theodoric died.

But it was not for long that the sacred edifice remained in Arian hands, for after Ravenna had been taken by the Byzantines, Archbishop Agnellus, between 556 and 565, consecrated the church for Catholic use after the edict issued by the Emperor Justinian giving to the « Sancta Mater Ecclesia Ravennae, vera Mater orthodoxa » all the property formely belonging to the Arians. After this « reconciliation » the church was dedicated to St. Martin, the famous Bishop who had fought against the heretics so vigorously as to be considered one of their bitterest foes, and to have earned himself the title of « Malleus Haereticorum » (Hammer of the heretics). It is thus obvious that a definite and deliberate intention animated Archbishop Agnellus in his choice of a Saint to whom to dedicate the basilica where once the Arian heretics had officiated.

But the name of St. Martin was also destined to fall into oblivion. This happened towards the middle of the 9th century, when, to save the sacred relics of St. Apollinaris, Ravenna's first Bishop, from the danger of profanation in one of the piratical invasions at the time frequent along the Adriatic coasts, it was decided to transfer—or to appear to transfer—the venerated bones of the saint from the splendid church at Classe to that of St. Martin which would be much safer because of its position within the walls of the city.

It was from this time that the church was usually called S. Apollinare, but with the addition still retained of « Nuovo » or « In Nowo » (new). This does not imply any distiction of chronological character between this church and S. Apollinare in Classe (which was built a few decades later than the Arian church) but is intended to disstinguish it from another of the city churches of the same name, but certainly smaller and more ancient, called « ad Monetam Veterem » and also « in Veclo ».

At one time there seems to have been an atrium before the façade of the church, which has been altered several times during the centuries. Today there is a simple and elegant portico with round arches, which was rebuilt in the 16th century. To the right stands a slender round *Campanile* more than 125 ft. high. It has windows with a single opening, others with two openings (« bifore ») and again others with three (« trifore »), and these help to relieve the solidity of the building which thus acquires an appearance of much greater lightness.

The *interior* of the church (about 138 ft. by 69 ft.) is divided into a central nave with two aisles by a double row of columns, 12 on each side. They are of Greek marble, and Greek ciphers and letters which are often repeated in different capitals, are often carved on them. They are evidently identification marks of the oriental work-shops in which the marbles were prepared. The capitals, all of corinthian type, are surmounted by « pulvini » which serve to separate the walls above still further from the columns.

The present flooring is about 4 ft. above the level of the original floor. The columns were all brought to their present level at the beginning of the 16th century, and as a result all the arches were lifted, to the detriment of one section of the wall, i.e. that which was originally between the cornice from which the mosaic decoration starts, and the line given by the upper part of the pulvini. It may be that in this lost part there was a decoration—not of inlaid marble (Rohault de Fleury) or of mosaic (Ricci) but of stuccos: these latter, in fact, are mentioned with satisfaction in Andrea-Agnello's « Liber Pontificalis ».

The apse at the further end of the church was rebuilt in 1950. It was raised on the very walls of the ancient building which were brought to light in that same year. The original apse was semicircular on the inside and pentagonal on the outside.

Before 1950 the church ended in a very deep baroque apse. Though damaged during the war it was still left standing in spite of the erection of the present apse. While the work for the erection of the new apse was in

S. Apollinare Nuovo: some figures of Prophets and, lower beneath, Theodoric's Palace on the south wall

S. Apollinare Nuovo: some figures of Prophets and, lower beneath, the town of Classe

S. Apollinare Nuovo: the Redeemer upon the throne with the Angels (detail)

progress, the crypt below the choir was explored. As it is always filled with water it can no longer be visited. Its form is that of a semianular ambulatory with barrel vaulting, to the centre of which is added a rectilineal corridor. It is of a type characteristic of the 9th century, but its erection must belong to the time of the actual or presumed transference of the bones of St. Apollinaris from the church at Classe outside the walls to this church.

While the earth was being removed from the outer walls in 1950 some small terracotta tubes pointed at one end were brought to light. Here we have the usual light material used in Ravenna for the construction of the domes of churches and apses; it is therefore not unreasonable to suppose that the dome of S. Apollinare Nuovo—which was gravely damaged by an earthquake in the days of Archbishop Giovanni V—was originally made of this special building material.

Close to the steps which lead from the central nave to the raised choir are placed three « transenne » i.e. large carved marble panels, and a pluteus, all these sculptures save one may be assigned to the 6th century and by their carved open-work, determined by the alternation of mass and space—and therefore of light and shade—they produce the typical black and white appearance which adds so greatly to their pictorial character.

The « pluteus », which is the first sculpture we meet on the left, shows on its front a vase from which spring two peacocks facing the monogrammatic cross between. Until 1950 it was inset in the wall of one of the chapels of the church; it was then removed in order to be given a more conspicuous position, and, for the first time, the ornamentation on the back was revealed. The decorative design unites here with a Biblical scene. Amid the trails of two great branches forming symmetrical coils Daniel appears in the attitude of prayer in the lions' den. The two loaves marked with a cross which are seen at the side near the Prophet's head stand for the food brought to Daniel by Habakkuk, while the dove with the crown in its beak signifies the divine intervention which has closed the lions' mouth.

The altar that stands in the centre of the choir has an aperture in front through which may be seen the base within, with spaces for the relics. It is of the 6th century. To the same age belong the porphyry columns of the ancient altar-canopy with their typical capitals two of which show the characteristic Byzantine open-work, while the other are Egyptian-Alexandrian.

The marble chair which stands behind is of the Roman period; it has a graceful plant decoration on its sides.

The marble pulpit also belongs the 6th century which rests upon the trunk of a solid column and stands between two of the columns of the nave. It has a curious ovoid shape. It has projecting cornices and is adorned with crosses in very flat relief standing upon globes.

In spite of the richness of the well balanced marble decoration and the serene composure of the interior, it must be stated that the sacred edifice is famous above all for the superb mosaics which cover the whole length of the walls of the central nave; and to think that originally this mantle of mosaic was even more extensive, for it covered also the apse and the inner façade! Moreover, the luminous gleam of the mosaic must have been still further enhanced by the fact that they were mirrored in the marbles which pannelled the side walls, in the stones of the flooring, and in the sunk panels of the roof, which we may reasonably conclude to have been gilded as the church was also described as « in coelo aureo ».

The existing mosaics may be divided into three horizontal zones: the first, or upper one, close to the roof (which in its present form with lacunars goes back to the early 17th century), consists of a series of decorative panels alternating with others—26 in all—showing scenes relating to the miracles and passion of Christ; the second, which covers the spaces between the windows, shows male figures in frontal position; the third, which fills the lowest zone, shows the procession of Martyrs and Virgins, and at the end the Palace of Theodoric and the City of Classe and the groups of Christ and the Madonna flanked by Angels.

It is not to be thought, however, that all the mosaic decoration belongs to the age of Theodoric. The greater part of it does indeed go back to that time but two large tracts certainly belong to the time of Justinian, and, to be more exact, to the time when Agnellus was Archbishop, for it was he who consecrated the church for Catholic worship. As the author of the « Liber Pontificalis Ecclesiae Ravennatis » tells us, to this period

S. Apollinare Nuovo: The Virgins

belong the sumptuous mosaics of the two processions—that of the Martyrs and that of the female Saints. The figures of the three Wise Men have also been incontestably shown to be of the same period.

Between the two decorations a period of about forty years elapsed. Though this is but a brief period it is sufficient to reveal a distinct difference of artistic manner between the two works for the mosaics of Theodoric's time, despite the use of the gold background, present figures with forceful outline, but, especially in the small panels above, they show a certain freedom of movement, together with a spontaneity and animation which are at times truly surprising.

The mosaics of Justinian's time show a composition bound together in rhythm that are repeated with a certain regularity, and cadences which recur at definite intervals.

In the panels showing *scenes of the miracles and passion of the Lord,* which extend, the one along the upper part of the left wall, and the other along the upper part of the

right wall, one notes that on the left, the scene generally has few figures and Christ is young and beardless, while on the right the personages are more crowded and Christ is a man of mature age and bearded.

These contrasts indicate not so much a difference in period, as has been thought, but rather a difference of hand; and perhaps we may also say that the artist who designed the cartoons for the panels on the right, had a more outstanding personality, since he reveals higher artistic gifts than the other who planned the decoration on the left.

Both on the right and on the left the scenes relating to the miracles and the passion begin at the further end of the church. The former series starts with the Marriage at Cana (but unfortunately the scene was altered when an unskilful restoration was carried out last century) and ends with the Healing of the paralytic; this has also been restored, for it was damaged by an Austrian bomb which fell upon the church in 1916, but this time the restoration was scrupulously carried out, careful at-

S.Apollinare Nuovo: Detail of the procession of Martyrs

tention being paid to photographs taken previously. All the other panels have come down to us in good state of preservation.

The *Marriage at Cana* is followed by the *Miracle of the Loaves and Fishes*. Next come the *Call of Peter and Andrew*, the *Healing of the Blind Men at Jericho*, and the *Healing of the Woman with the Issue of Blood*. The next scenes are: The *Samaritan Woman at the Well*, the *Raising of Lazarus*, the *Pharisee and the Publican at the Temple gate*, and the *Widow offering her Mite*. Lastly, after the scene of the *Separation of the Good from the Bad*, symbolically expressed by two groups, one of sheep, the other of goats, flanked respectively by the Angel of Good, clad in red and the Angel of Evil in blue, come three more miracles: The *Cure at Capernaum of the Paralytic* who is let down through the open roof into the presence of Jesus, the *Healing of the Man possessed of a devil* and the *Cure of the Paralysed Man at Bethesda.*

The scenes of Christ's Passion begin with the Last Supper and end with the Unbelief of St. Thomas. The picture of the *Last Supper* closely resembles in composition an illumination in the famous Greek Evangelistery known as the «Codex Purpureus» which is of the 6th century and is preserved in the Cathedral of Rossano. Then comes *Jesus on the Mount of Olives*, followed by the *Kiss of Judas*, *Christ before Caiaphas*, *Jesus tells Peter he will deny him*, *Peter's Denial*. Next comes the *Remorse of Judas*, and then *Pilate washes his hands*, and *Jesus on his way to Calvary*. Finally one sees the *Three Maries at the Tomb*, the *Walk to Emmaus*, and the *Unbelief of St. Thomas*.

The mosaics between the windows show only male figures—32 in all—in frontal position and holding a scroll or book. They are probably *Prophets*. The design is clear and the modelling fully preserves the sense

S. Apollinare Nuovo: Marble « pluteo »

of volume; all this goes to prove that the mosaicist still adhered to the Hellenistico-Roman artistic tradition.

We cannot say the same for the two admirable *Processions of Martyrs and Virgins*, who, with their slow advance, incessantly repeat the same vertical rhythms, so that their unvarying modulation at once recalls the Byzantine scheme of composition in which one finds over and over again the repetition of the same motif. It is almost like the recitation of so many verses of a Psalm succeeding one another with the same length and the same pauses; it is almost like the monotonous succession of invocations in two long litanies. Indeed one may say at once that these two slow Processions are nothing but two pictorial litanies, for above the head of every Martyr and every Virgin the name is written.

All the personages are similarly dressed. But the embroidered gold tunics and white veils of the Virgins surpass in richness and splendour the white mantles of the Martyrs led by St. Martin who is the only one to wear a purple cloak.

The Virgins, preceded by the *Three Wise Men* (the upper parts of which have been completely renewed in a recent restoration) move towards the *Madonna with the Child Jesus* on her knee. The Martyrs advance towards *Christ enthroned*, with two Angels on each side. These two groups show such a sense of hieratic dignity that it has been supposed that the artist who planned the composition must have been somewhat influenced by formal oriental schemes.

The representation of the *Palace of Theodoric*, at the beginning of the right wall is curious, not only because some have thought to see here a reproduction in open perspective, of the church prepared for ceremonies (Dyggve), but also because traces are even now visible of a « purge » in the figu-

*S. Apollinare Nuovo:
« Transenna »
large carved
marble*

res of those personages who had originally been represented on the spaces between the columns of the portico. In fact, some hands belonging to these figures can still be seen at the height of about half the length of the columns. Clearly visible too are the semicircular outlines of the heads above the horizontal spears supporting the curtains which Archbishop Agnellus put in place of those figures which very probably representing dignitaries of the Gothic King's Court.

A similar « damnatio memoriae », or « purge » took place also in the case of other figures at one time standing out against the walls of the City of Classe which, with its neighbouring Port, is represented on the opposite wall. There is no doubt that when the basilica was « reconciled » for Catholic worship, the memory of these persons was no longer acceptable.

On the inner façade of the church we now see a rectangular fragment of mosaic showing a *personage with diadem and nimbus, clad in tunic and mantle.* The inscription above names him Justinian, but the inscription was added in a restoration carried out by Kibel in the second half of the last century. Considering the difference between this face and that of Justinian in the apse of St. Vitale, some have thought that this may be the mutilated remains of a mosaic with the portrait of King Theodoric (Priess, Lorentz).

Bishop Maximian, whose fortunate lot it had been to consecrate S. Vitale, shortly afterwards—on May 9th, 549—also consecrated the large imposing basilica of S. Apollinare in Classe. The name « in Classe » derives from the neighbouring « oppidum Classis », the town which sprang up in defence of the famous Port founded by Augustus. And it was to the inhabitants of this « castrum » or fort, who were mainly merchants and seamen, that S. Apollinaris, the first Bishop of Ravenna, brought the good tidings of the new Faith, the comforting words of the Gospel. We do not know exactly when he lived: it is hardly likely that we must go back so far as the age of the Apostles, as is suggested in the « Passio S. Apollinaris », a legendary narrative drawn up probably at the end of the 5th or at the beginning of the 6th century (Mazzotti). The desire to go back to this ancient time shows that the hagiographer, while wishing to ennoble the figure of the first Bishop, tried at the same time to shed further glory upon the origin of the church of his city.

Very soon cemeteries arose around the town of Classe, and these were in part used by the Christians, as can be proved from the discovery there of various funerary inscriptions. Beside, rather than upon one of these burying grounds, as De Rossi has thought, Bishop Ursicinus, in the second quarter of the 6th century, built the magnificent church of Classe which now stands almost alone (at least for the present) in the midst of the country, whilst behind it, towards the sea, stretches the dark green of that vast pine wood « spessa e viva » (thick and living) of which Dante and Byron sang.

The Church is about four miles from the centre of Ravenna, and is now far from the sea which was at one time very near it. It can be seen from afar, not so much because of its imposing mass, but for the tall and massive *Campanile* (123 ft. high),

S. Apollinare in Classe: Sarcophagus of the Archbishop Theodore

belonging perhaps to the end of the 10th century, which is rendered more slender and graceful in appearance by the ascending series of windows—the lowest with a single opening (« monofore »), the next above with two openings (« bifore »), and the third with three (« trifore »). In these latter there are white columns with characteristic crutch-shaped capitals.

Julianus Argentarius, who financed the construction of S. Vitale, undertook the considerable task of building this church too, and it is for that reason that one sees here the long thin red bricks which are to be seen in all Julianus's other edifices.

This church, which has the usual basilican form, at first had an atrium in front of it, as is proved by the fact that some remains of it were discovered last century. To the central block of the façade, flanked on their side by two smooth uprights, is added the narthex which has on its left a high quadrangular building which has been a great deal restored. There must also have been a similar structure on the right, for it has been possible to trace its foundations.

A rhythmical design of blind arches sup-ported by uprights enlivens the side walls of the exterior, in which there are numerous wide windows. The apse, semicircular inside, is polygonal outside. Beside the apse stand the two square chapels known as the « prothesis » and the « diaconicon », each of which has a small pentagonal apse.

The *interior* (182 ft. by 99 ft.) is spacious and solemn, and is impressive especially for the great width of the central nave, which is flanked by two rows of magnificent marble columns from the workshops of Proconnesos. They are marked by horizontal veining, are raised upon square bases and are surmounted by capitals carved with leaves that seem blown out by the wind. Above the capitals are « pulvini ». The whole of this material shows the most homogeneous uniformity of style and measurement, so that there is no doubt that it was expressly ordered for the erection of this church.

The side walls, in each of which there were originally three doors, are now a bare and unadorned expanse of brick, but once they were covered with panels of polished marble, for Andrea-Agnello writes in his « Liber Pontificalis Ecclesiae Ravennatis », that no church in Italy was so rich in valuable stones—« in lapidibus preciosis »—. These marbles were in great part carried away in the first half of the 15th century when Sigismondo Pandolfo Malatesta asked for and obtained them to decorate the church at Rimini which took its name from him.

The choir of the church is now raised well above the level of the nave: this is due to the addition below it of the crypt, which is semicircular in form with a central corridor. Some critics think it was built in the 7th century (Grabar), according to others (Mazzotti) towards the end of the 9th, while yet others (Ricci) attribute it to the second half of the 12th. In any case it is certain that when the basilica was built, instead of the raised choir, there was the « bema », or enclosure reserved for the clergy; this extended towards the centre of the edifice as far as the two third columns from the further end. In fact, its foundations—upon which must have rested the carved sections and small marble pilastres for the parapet surrounding it—were brought to light in 1953 about one foot below the level of the present flooring, as the result of certain careful investigations.

Of the ancient mosaic flooring which must have covered the whole of this vast building like an immense carpet, a few remains have been found at the end of the left aisle, and at the beginning of the right. Here an expanse of mosaic, showing geometrical designs, preserves an inscription recording that a great part of this work was done at her personal expense by a certain lady « Gaudentia », and a certain « Felix », together with other benefactors. Another fragment of mosaic, discovered in 1953 below the flooring of the central nave, has been affixed to the right wall of the church.

But the thing which most attracts the attention of the visitor as he enters the church of S. Apollinare in Classe, is without doubt the sumptuous many-coloured mantle of mosaic which covers the *choir arch* and the *semidome of the apse*.

Not all this mosaic, however, belongs to the same period. The upper part of the arch would seem to go back, according to some scholars (Toesca) to the 9th century, but according to others (Galassi) it is to be attributed to the 9th. In the upper part, which stretches horizontally over the whole width above the arch, is a figure of *Christ* with wide open eyes and wrinkled brow,

within a medaillon. Beside him, in the midst of a sea of stylised clouds, are the *winged symbols of the Evangelists*, the Eagle, the Man, the Lion and the Bull; in the last figure it is to be noticed that the head is drawn strictly in profile but the nostrils appear to be in a perfectly frontal position. The zone below these figures shows on the extreme right and left the two symbolical *cities of Jerusalem and Bethlehem*, their walls adorned with precious stones. From their gates issue *twelve lambs*, six on each side, which advance upwards towards the Christ in the medaillon above; we have here undoubtedly a symbolic representation of the twelve Apostles.

In the narrow spaces beside the arch two palm trees stand out on a dark blue background. This part of the mosaic is to be assigned to the 6th century, as are also the figures below representing the *Archangels Gabriel and Michael*, who, like celestial warriors, carry the « labarum » or banner bearing the praise of the Thrice Holy God. Lower still we see the figures belonging to the 12th century (Toesca) of *St. Matthew* and, perhaps, *St. Luke*.

The entire decoration of the dome of the apse is to be attributed to about the middle of the 6th century. The composition, based on the agreement of colours few but bright, falls naturally into two parts. Above, upon a sky of gold streaked by many small clouds, stands a great jewelled disc which contains a cross studded with many precious stones; this, in its turn, at the point where the arms cross, bears, within a circle, the head of Christ. The upper part of the cross is surmounted by the Greek word IXΘYC; the word means « fish » and the letters of the Greek word stand for the initial letters of « Jesus Christ Son of God Saviour ». Beneath the cross we read the words: « Salus Mundi » i.e. Salvation of the World.

This great medaillon is flanked by the figures of *Moses* and *Elijah* emerging from the clouds. Their presence clearly proves that the artist is alluding to the Transfiguration of Christ on Mt. Tabor, which was witnessed by the Apostles Peter, James and John, whom we must recognize as being represented symbolically by the *three lambs* which stand below but raise their heads towards the jewelled cross.

Lower down the zone widens out into a green flowery valley, varied by the emergence of small dark rocks bordered with white, and enlivened by a luxuriant growth of grass, bushes and other plants among which we may see the pine—the tree which is still today especially characteristic of the countryside around Ravenna. In the centre of this scene, which has a soft shade of green for background, stands the tall, solemn imposing figure of *St. Apollinaris* wearing, over his white alb, the chasuble adorned with many golden bees—the symbol of eloquence. The first Bishop of Ravenna is in the attitude of an « orans » i.e. he is pictured at the moment of uttering his prayer that God will grant his heavenly grace to the faithful entrusted to his care who are here seen as *twelve lambs* that surround him. It is for this reason that the composition might almost be said to be inspired by the last words of the sermon which St. Peter Chrysologus preached in honour of St. Apollinaris: « Ecce vivit, ecce ut bonus Pastor suo medio assistit in grege » (Behold he lives, behold how the good Shepherd stands in the midst of his flock).

The figures of the Bishops Severus, Ecclesius, Ursus and Ursicinus clad in their sacred vestments, which are seen in the spaces between the windows, are contemporary with the building of the church.

The two panels seen at the side of the apse are a little more that a century later: in the right we see the *Sacrifices of Abel, Abraham and Melchizedeck* where the composition is not devoid of balance, but the colours are weak and undecided. On the left are the *Emperor Constantine IV Pogonatus (the bearded) with his brothers Heraclius and Tiberius in the act of handing the rescript of « Privileges » to Reparatus, the delegate of Archbishop Maurus.* The work reechoes the one seen on the panels of the apse of S. Vitale, but during the course of centuries, it has undergone various alterations, so that today we see it almost all restored in tempera to imitate mosaic.

There are some important *sarcophagi* lining the side walls of the church. They belong to the 5th, 6th, 7th and 8th centuries, and by taking them in turn one can gain an idea of the development of sculpture throughout this period. One notices how, from the sculptured figures of the Apostles which in the art of Ravenna are typical of the 5th century one passes in the next century and those that follow, to representations in which their symbolical and decorative character is increased by the lack of modelling, and indeed by a very marked flatness.

Also worthy of note is the *marble canopy* over the altar at the further end of the left aisle; from the inscription around the upper border we learn that it was erected at the beginning of the 9th century in honour of the third Bishop of Ravenna St. Eleucadius. Beneath the canopy, and affixed to the wall, are two small marble panels showing the *Annunciation;* in one the Angel advances with his staff and stretching out his hand as he speaks; in the other the Virgin is seen seated in the act of spinning purple thread. These two small panels are to be assigned, not so much to the 7th century as some have said (Gerspach), as to the 10th.

S. Apollinare in Classe:
The marble ciborium

This mausoleum with its austere and ponderous mass, stands alone in the midst of a group of dark cypress trees, rather less than a mile from the centre of the city, on the furthest verge of the « Campo Coriandro », in a region which the Goths had used as a burying ground, as one concludes from discoveries made on the spot during the last century.

A writer who lived shortly after Theodoric and is known by the name of « Anonimo Valesiano » gives us the important information that the Gothic King « while still living raised to himself a monument built

Theodoric's portrait on the gold medallion coming from Senigallia now in the National Roman Museum

of great squared blocks, to cover which he sought an immense stone ».

And in fact this imposing tomb is built of great blocks of Istrian stone, perfectly squared and securely joined together. It consists of two parts, the one above the other. The lower part is decagonal, and on every side there is a wide and deep niche having a round arch formed of large wedge-shaped stones. In the niche facing west there is a door leading into the interior which is in the form of a cross with cross vaulting, and is lighted by six small windows with wide embrasures that enable one to judge the very considerable thickness of the walls. On the two blocks that jut out from the wall at the further end two shells are carved. From the wall opposite to these, two other masses project: one is still in its rough state, while the other repeats the shell which is, however, merely sketched. It is interesting to notice that the angles of the building are not formed by the conjunction of mutually supporting blocks of stone, but the corner stones were placed in position after having been cut to form the angle.

The upper storey, though somewhat smaller, is also decagonal, but the interior is perfectly circular. On each of the outer walls, except the one with the door, we may see outlines of two rectangular recesses, each surmounted by a lunette in relief. Above this zone the building becomes circular, and on its surface there is a frieze showing a motif suggestive of a pair of pincers.

Upon this circular band rests the massive cover which consists of a huge monolith of Istrian stone measuring about 36 ft. in diameter, and nearly 10 ft. in height. It is believed to weigh about three hundred Italian tons. Along the outer edge of this monolith are carved, at equal distances from one another, twelve « handles », under each of which there is a gap. The usual opinion is that through these holes the ropes were passed by means of which it was possible to carry out the difficult task of raising the mass, with the help, probably of an inclined plane.

One of the problems which have most wearied scholars is that which relates to the original appearance of the upper storey, and of the manner in which the lower and the upper parts were connected.

Some have thought that all round the upper part there was a sort of covered gallery supported by slender columns (Vandelli, Ginanni); another has thought that at the sides of the decagon there were two arched niches jutting outward and supported by slender columns (Schulz); again, it has been suggested that originally all the sides were quite smooth, and that is was only later that the rectangular recesses and lunettes were added (Durm); it has also been maintained that the original plan was to carry the decagonal form up to and including the roof (Fiechter) and that it was only the possibility of making use of a great monolith which caused the project to be modified (Cecchelli). Finally the theory has been advanced—and it seems the most probable—that on each face of the decagon there was a decoration of simple pensile arches (Ricci, Guberti) which some consider was never completed (Haupt, Gerola).

With regards to the heterogeneous circular cap of the mausoleum set upon a recagonal body, Ferry has recently made some remarkable observations, and has given a singular explanation for various decorative and architectural features to which earlier scholars had not paid very much attention. Thus, Ferri thought that the upper part of the monument—contrarily to the laws of functionality in the Roman architectural tradition—was made circular, because Theodoric desired that his tomb should have, at least in the upper part, the form of the tents in use among his ancestors. It is for this reason that Ferri sees in the frieze with its pincers-like design, not merely an ornamental element typical of northern art, but the translation into stone of a functional object of metal, i.e. the four hooks moving in opposite directions united with a pivot so as to form a cross; these hooks so operated as to facilitate the passage into and out of the tent that was made up of several widths of canvas; these, in order the better to be seen, have not been shown hanging straight down as they would normally appear, but with a rotation of 90 degrees.

Ferri found support for this brilliant theory of his in the presence of other elements which, now translated into stone, no longer have the functional character which was originally theirs. For example, he considers that the twelve modillions upon the edge of the cap—on the outer faces of which are carved the names of the four Evangelists and eight of the Apostles—were not so planned as to supply a means of raising the enormous monolith, but in order to reproduce the appearance of the top of a tent supported upon strong poles, which, radiating from the centre, reached the circumference and then projected from it each forming a hook.

Proceeding still further along these lines, Ferri sees in the cross painted upon the summit of the ceiling of the enormous cap, a motif, well suited certainly to a sepulchral chamber, but a structure corresponding to the « decussatio viminea » of the Asiatic tents, in which two poles laid at right angles one to another were crossed by a circular opening to let out the smoke; this opening was closed during the night and in wet weather by a large disc, and this has been reproduced on the exterior of the mausoleum in the great central disc which is about 12 ft. in diameter, and overlaps the rest by about four inches.

These twelve modillions could certainly never have supported statues, as has been thought (Fabbri), for on their upper part they are not level, but for some scholars they have recalled « materially the armed head of a warrior, and symbolically the savage might of war » (Guberti).

On entering the upper storey of the monument, one sees in the centre a large porphyry coffin; it must at one time have contained the Gothic King's remains which were later lost. Then, on gazing up from the inside at the great monolith, one is clearly able to see on one side a crack reaching almost to the top. It is exceedingly likely that it was caused by a jolt when the stone was being lifted into place, but a legend handed down in Ravenna from generation to generation offers another explanation. It is said among the people that the crack was caused when a lightning struck the building, on the very day when Theodoric, whose death by lightning had been foretold to him, had taken refuge there during a terrible storm. But in spite of this, the lightning, cleaving its way through the mighty stone, struck the Arian King and reduced his body to ashes.

The Archiepiscopal Museum is situated on the first floor of the Archiepiscopal Palace: the material collected there comes above all from the old Cathedral « Ursiana » which was destroyed in the XVIII century. The mosaic fragments here come from the apsidal motif of the church and show the Virgin Mary at prayer and the heads of St. John, the Evangelist, St. Peter, S. Barbazian, S. Ursicino and a soldier, and are fixed to the wall of the first room. Below these fragments are the marble transennae probably of the VI cent.

On the opposite wall, in the centre, is a part of the marble ambo from the church of St. John and St. Paul, which is characterized by a series of panels forming diverse overlapping folds each of which surrounds the figure of an extremely flat animal. The inscription running along the top frame is considered to be of the Marinian episcopacy, towards the end of the VI cent.

In the first room there are some capitals, considered by some to be of the VI century, and by others, of the V. These capitals are decorated with animal-forms. Very notable is the small rectangular marble « capsella », of the V century. Its four sides show the following: Daniel in the lion's den, the adoration of the kings, the women at the Tomb, the Ascension, and lastly the delivering of the Commandments. Under the entrance archway of the second room, in 1961, a Greek marble sarcophagus was placed. This sarcophagus, was for two hundred years enclosed in the high altar of the Cathedral. The sarcophagus belongs to the end of the V century or beginning of the VI and is of the type called « columned » because each of its four sides contain a series of niches, the whole of it crowned by shells and supported by columns. The remaining walls of the room contain Christian funeral inscriptions in Latin, the oldest found in Ravenna.

In the centre of the second room on the walls of which some Roman epigraphs and bas-reliefs may be seen there is a beautiful porphyry statue. Unfortunately the head was missing when it was found. It is of an Emperor of the late imperial age in the act of replacing his sword into its scabbard.

In some of the cases at the far end of a corridor some very interesting pieces of material are kept. More noteworthy than the purple coloured veil and the VII - VIII century fragments of episcopal girdles, found in 1940 in a sarcophagus in the right hand apse of St. Apollinaris in Classe, is the great chasuble called « Angelopte » of the last half of the XII century.

This very fine chasuble is in dark-blue coloured brocade and adorned with quarter moons and small eagles. In a small circular adjoining room there is the rarest relic in the museum: the famous ivory throne of Archbishop Maximian who was archbishop of Ravenna towards the end of the first

Archiepiscopal Museum: Marble chest with the scene of the Magi offering their gifts

half of the VI century. It is thought that this throne was probably donated by the Emperor Justinian himself.

On the front panel among the decorative motifs, are the four Evangelists and John the Baptist, on the back are scenes from the life of Jesus, some of which are inspired by the canonical texts. On the rear panels are episodes from the life of Joseph.

The scholars are divided about the origins of this masterpiece of carving, which clearly shows the hands of different artists; some think it was carved at Alexandria, others at Constantinople and some even think it was carved in Ravenna itself.

To reach the chapel one crosses the rooms of the Episcopal Museum. This chapel was erected by a certain Archbishop Peter: but probably not Peter I or III (570-578), as was until recently thought, but Peter II who was archbishop from 494 to 519, thus in the full Theodorian period.

The chapel is behind a small rectangular atrium bearing on its walls painted imitations of mosaics. Some traces of the original still remain and are described in twenty Latin hexameters thanks to the transcription of the historian A. Agnello in the IX century. The first of these is very significant because it underlines poetically the light given out by the mosaics: *Aut lux hic nata est capta hic libera regnat* («light is born here, or made prisoner and here reigns freely»).

Over the door is the figure of the Warrior Christ: the bottom half is a complete restoration but was traced on a secure base, showing Christ's head with a halo and cross dressed in armour and cloak. He appears full faced in the act of trampling on the neck of a lion and a serpent, symbols of the powers of evil. In his right hand he is holding a long cross resting on his shoulder, and in his left an open book, on the pages of which can be seen the words he spoke describing himself: *Ego sum via, veritas et vita* (I am the way, truth and life).

The Oratory itself, in the form of a cross, ends in a small apse, the dome of which, now completely painted in tempera, represents the sky at night with a cross in the centre. The dome is gold with the monogram of Christ, formed by the intertwined Greek letters, I (iota) and χ (chi) signifying Jesus Christ. This monogram is shown supported by four angels lined along the rib-structure of the vault ceiling itself.

Between the angels supporting the monogram are the four winged symbols of the Evangelists emerging from coloured clouds, the Eagle (St. John), Man (St. Matthew), the Calf (St. Luke), the Lion (St. Mark). Under the eastern and western archways, within circular medallions are busts of the apostles on each side of the bust of Christ: under the northern and southern archways are the busts of six male and six female saints (the former partly restored).

The six female saints with gems in their hair and around their necks are embellished by a white silk veil, adorned with precious stones which from their heads, falls over and behind their shoulders. In the chapel one may see the precious silver cross called « Agnello cross » after the archbishop who had it made for him during his episcopacy, between 557 and 570 A.D.

All the four arms of the cross, are decorated with circular medallions containing busts of the saints. Some of these were restored in the XVI century, especially the ones on the lower arm. The medallions containing the Virgin Praying, on one side, and the Resurrection on the other, at the highest point of the cross, were done about this period.

Archiepiscopal Museum: Ivory throne of Maximian (detail)

The ancient building commonly called the Palace of Theodoric stands close to the church of S. Apollinare Nuovo. Little more than the façade of it now remains. It certainly is not Theodoric's Palace for it is well known that the King's Palace stood behind the Arian church, and in the early decades of this century Ghirardini unearthed its foundations and reconstructed its plan.

Scholars do not agree in their efforts to fix the age of this building, or to decide its original purpose. The façade has three distinct parts; the central part has a lofty portal right above which is a large niche in the form of a balcony. The parts which flank the central mass are perfectly symmetrical: below, on each side is an opening with a double arch, and high above it is a blind loggia with three columns resting on a marble bracket. The façade is flanked on both sides by an an upright rising almost to the roof below which it forms part of the first arch of the blind loggia.

Some have thought that this building is to be identified as the Guard Room called in ancient times « Calchi », and have assigned it to the end of the 7th, or the beginning of the 8th century (Ricci); others have considered it to be the « Sicreston » or secretarial office of the Exarchs, and have attributed it to the first half of the 8th century (Galassi); others again, and perhaps more reasonably, think that it is the façade of the narthex of the Church of S. Salvatore (Gerola, Verzone); in this case the two small towers with their stairways flanking it at the back would have served merely to give access to the upper galleries or « matroneum » that must have extended above the aisles of the church which (as the excavations have proved) had a central nave, two aisles and a large apse.

However these things may be, it is certain that the architecture of this building, despite the use made of material from earlier edifices, shows such innovations, when compared with other buildings, as to bear witness to the fact that it belongs to a new artistic period.

The so-called Palace of Theodoric

THE TOMB OF DANTE

Towards the end of Via Dante just at the bottom, rises the Tomb of the Great Poet, who died, in exile at Ravenna, on the night between 13th and 14th September 1321.

The small and modest construction, of a sober neoclassic style, was built in 1780 by C. Morigia at the wishes of the Cardinal Legate, L. Valenti Gonzaga, whose coat-of-arms surmounts the door.

On the wall facing the door on entering, lined with marble is the sepulchre containing Dante's bones. The chest bears a Latin epitaph by B. Canaccio carved in 1327.

The English translation is as follows: « The rights of monarchy, the heavens and infernal lakes of the Phlegethon that I visited I sang, as long as mortal destiny decreed. But my soul was taken to a better place and reached its creator among the stars. Here I lie buried, Dante, exile from my birth-place. a son of Florence, that loveless mother ».

And above the chest is a golden cross given by Pope Paul VI on the occasion of the seven hundredth anniversary of the birth of the poet, and just below is the bas-relief carved by P. Lombardi in 1483, representing a thoughtful Dante at a lectern.

At the foot of the chest since 1921 one can see the bronze wreath placed there by the victorious Italian army of the first world war. From the middle of the domed ceiling hangs a small votive lamp, the oil for which comes from the Tuscany hills and is presented on every anniversary by the Florence town council.

Towards the end of the XV century Bernard Bembo, Venetian lord of Ravenna moved Dante's tomb to the western wall of one of the quiet Franciscan cloisters from which the monks by working a hole from the inside of the wall removed the poet's bones in 1519, thus avoiding their transfer to Florence, ordered by the Medici Pope Leone X.

The bones were jealously kept hidden in the Franciscan monastery near the evergreen garden of the Braccioforte quadrangle, until 1865 when they were found. Under the arches of « Braccioforte » the ex-oratorium, there are two very antique marble sarcophagi. One of these, of the V century, is very interesting with its four carved panels, which were described by G. D'Annunzio in his « Francesca da Rimini ».

The redeemer
Has a lion and a serpent under foot;
Elizabeth visits Mary;
The angel appears to the blessed Virgin;
Deer quenching their thirst at a spring.

The opening of the picture gallery in Ravenna dates back to 1829. The collection of several works of art was carried out through the appeal which the vice-Legate Mons. Livinio de' Medici Spada, Ignazio Sarti, the Gonfalonier Conte Carlo Arrigoni addressed to all the inhabitants of Ravenna, and by the Cardinal Legate Agostino Rivarola's authoritative permission.

Most of Ravenna's nobles immediately answered that fair call. Planned by Ignazio Sarti and built in Via Baccarini, it became the seat for the fine arts Academy a few years later. Recently all the works of art and the Academy itself have been transferred to the « Loggia del Giardino », called « Loggetta Lombardesca ».

In this splendid monumental whole, enriched with a large brick building on each side, a superimposed order arcade formed by five quick and harmonious spans, stands out for its pretty shape.

It is the « Loggetta Lombardesca », so called for its having been worked on mainly by lombard marble-cutters of the early sixteenth century.

Placed behind it is the large, double-arched cloister of the former S. Maria in Porto Monastery, built in the early sixteenth century.

The number of paintings displayed in the Academy Gallery dates back from thirteenth to twentieth century.

Also to be particularly noted are the paintings by artists from the Romagnola school, such as Nicolò Rondinelli, a Renaissance painter follower of Giovanni Bellini and author of a beautiful altar-piece representing the Virgin Mary between S. Caterina and S. Girolamo, crowned by two angels; Francesco Zaganelli from Cotignola, an early seventeenth century artist, with his original « Shepherds' Worship »; Luca Longhi who portrayed Captain Raffaele Rasponi and doctor Giovanni Arrigoni in the second half of XVI century.

Among the valuable pictures from other schools you can find Guercino's « S. Romualdo », Palmezzano's Nativity, Presentation to the temple, Ludovico Carracci's Christ's head, Antonio Vivarini's Crucifixion.

The marble statue of the soldier Guidarello Guidarelli, who died in 1501 at Imola, is placed within a large hall with fine paintings.

The work was done by Tullio Lombardi in 1525 and first of all is noteworthy for its features' delicacy contrasting with the stiffness of the armour enclosing the whole body.

As D'Annunzio wrote in his Laudi, the young knight was represented:
... asleep lying on his back with folded arms on his wide sword.
His motionless face bore the seal of iron, death and suffering...

Academy Gallery: Guidarello Guidarelli (detail)

This large well contained rectangular square marks the centre of the town, not only in its position, but because it has many public buildings overlooking it, for example the Town-Hall and Prefecture.

The oldest and most characteristic part is on the south west, where the Town-Hall forms a corner with the Venetian Palace, and two high columns have stood nearby since 1483.

The Venetions surmounted these columns with statues of St. Apollinare, first Bishop of Ravenna and the Lion of S. Marco.

The latter was substituted by a statue of St. Vitale in 1509. The circular pedestals in the form of steps on which P. Lombardi carved elegant decorative motifs, are very characteristic.

The Town Hall was built in 1400 but almost completely rebuilt in 1681, and some of the exterior decoration, such as the window ornaments and heavy battlements were added during the last century. Two very interesting points are to be noted in the rather low but wide porticoes on the lower part and, higher, the round ocular openings above the windows.

The Venetian Palace, erected during the second half of the XV century also has a series of very wide and airy porticoes on the lower part, over which stand beautiful white columned mullioned windows and a small balcony.

It is interesting to note how the granite columns of the porticoes are crowned by capitals decorated with acanthus leaves and on four of them King Theodoric's monogram is carved; they come from the church of St. Andrew of the Goths, which was destroyed by the Venetians during their dominion over the city.

COLOUR PLATES

Mausoleum of Galla Placidia: Interior

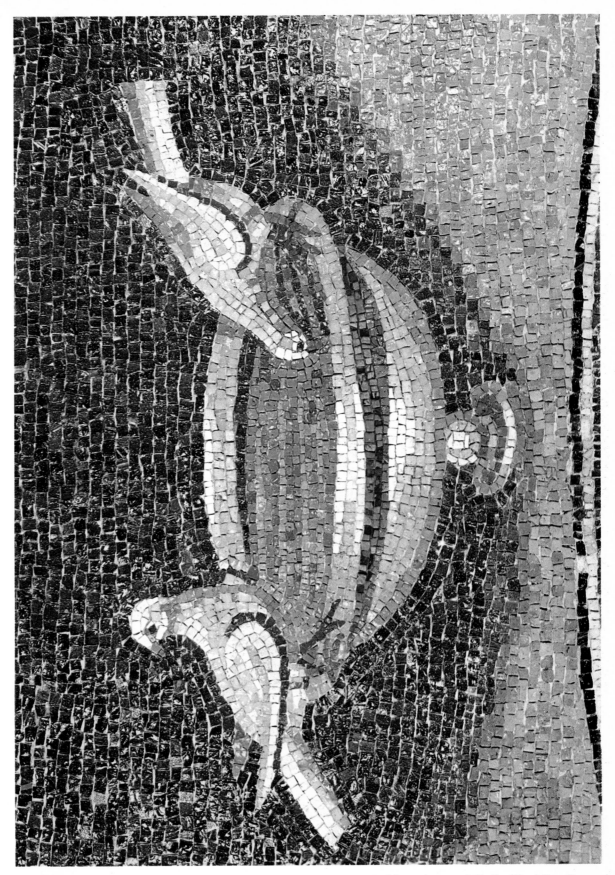

Mausoleum of Galla Placidia: Doves

Mausoleum of Galla Placidia: Mosaics of the vault

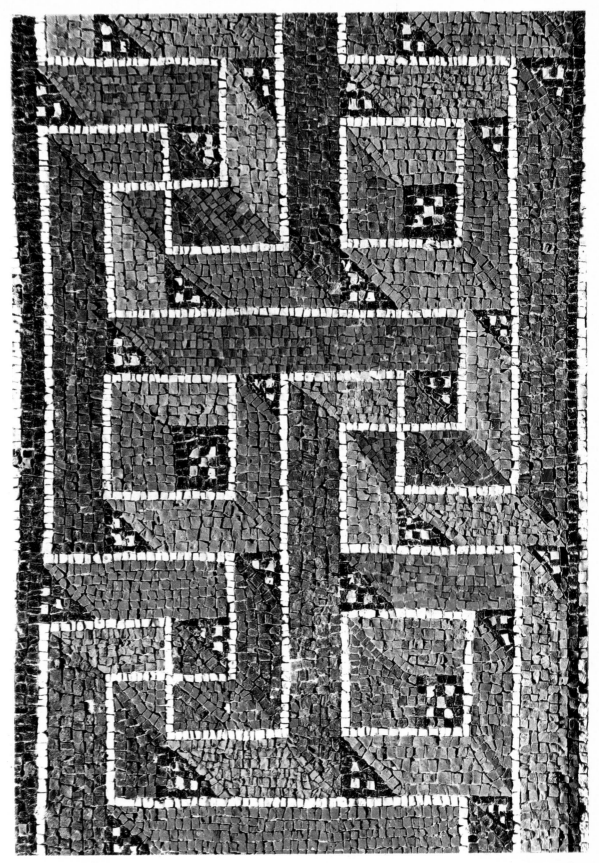

Mausoleum of Galla Placidia: Detail of the Greek Fret

Mausoleum of Galla Placidia:
The Good Shepherd

Mausoleum of Galla Placidia:
Detail of the decoration

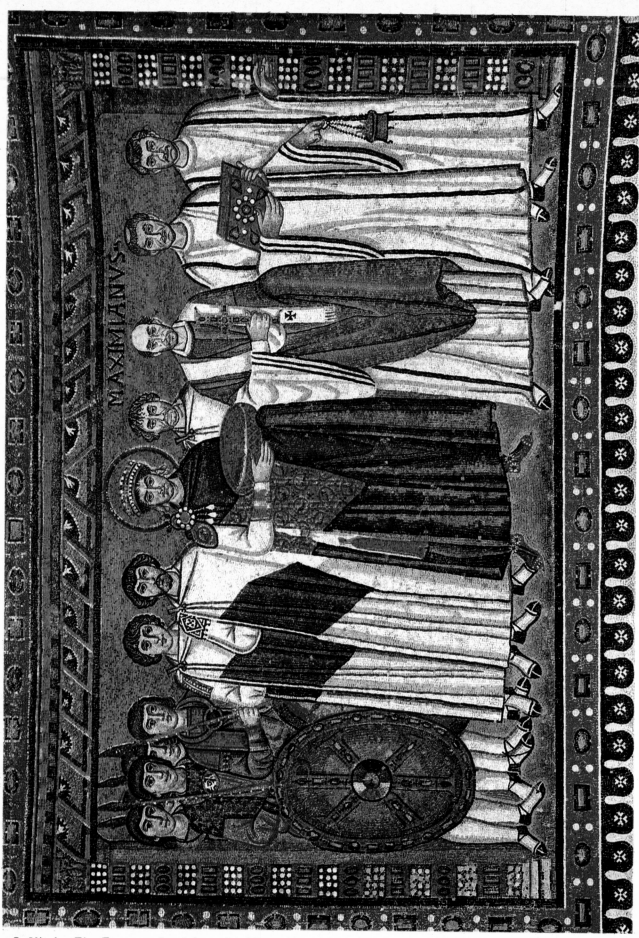

S. Vitale: The Emperor Justinian with his retinue

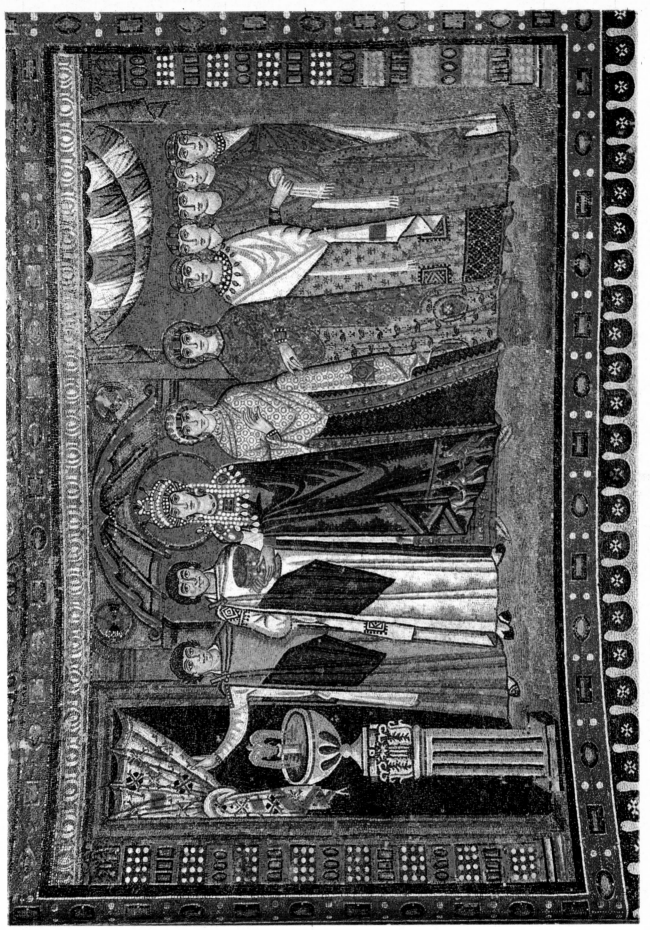

73   *S. Vitale: The Empress Theodora with her Court*

S. Vitale: The Emperor Justinian

74

S. Vitale: The Empress Theodora

S. Vitale:
Hospitality
of Abraham (detail)

S. Vitale:
Hospitality of Abraham
and sacrifice of Isaac

ECLESIVSEPS

SCSVITALIS

S. Vitale: The mosaic decoration in the apse

S. Vitale: A capital

S. Vital: Symbol of St. Luke the Evangelist

S. Vitale: Symbol of St. Mark the Evangelist

S. Vitale:
The Hebrews
at the foot
of Mount Sinai

S. Vitale: Decoration of the Presbytery

S. Vitale:
Detail of the vault
of the Presbytery

S. Vitale: Abel, detail of the Presbytory

S. Vitale: Melchizedek, detail of the Presbytery

*S. Vitale:
The sacrifices
of Abel
and Melchizede*

*S. Vitale:
Decoration
of the Presbyte*

S. Vitale: *Decoration of the Presbytery*

S. Vitale:
Detail of the triumphal arch

S. Vitale: Interior

S. Vitale:
Detail of the triumphal arch ▷

S. Vitale: Decoration of the Presbytery

90

Cathedral Baptistry: Stucco decoration and mosaics of the dome

Cathedral Baptistry: The baptism of Christ

⇦
Arian Baptistry:
Detail of the dome

Arian Baptistry:
Detail of the dome

Arian Baptistry: Mosaics of the dome

EVLALIA✝SCAAGNES✝   ✝SCAAGATHES✝SCAPELAC

S. Apollinare Nuovo: The Virgins

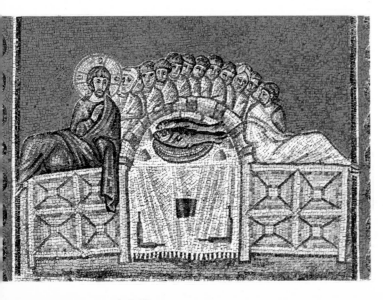

S. Apollinare Nuovo:
The Last Supper

S. Apollinare Nuovo:
Interior ⇨

95

S. Apollinare Nuovo: *The three Magi*

S. Apollinare Nuovo:
*Our Lady upon the throne
with the Angels*

SCS·MARTINVS✝SCS·CLEMIS✝SCS·SVSTVS✝SCS·LAVRENTIVS

S. Apollinare Nuovo: The procession of Martyrs

S. Apollinare Nuovo:
The Redeemer upon the throne
with the Angels

S. Apollinare Nuovo: The call of Peter and Andrew (detail)

*S. Apollinare
Nuovo:
The call
of Peter
and Andrew*

S. Apollinare Nuovo: Resurrection of Lazarus

S. Apollinare Nuovo: The Woman of Samaria at the well

S. Apollinare Nuovo: Christ as judge separating the sheep from the goats

*S. Apollinare Nuovo:
The mosaic decorati
of the North wall
(detail)*

102

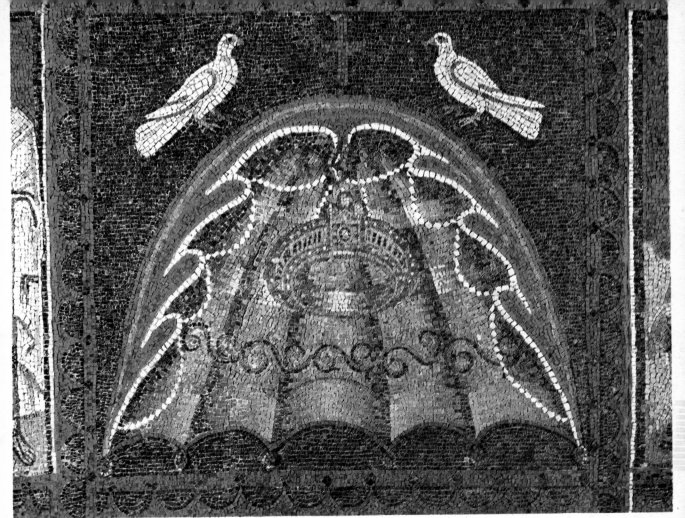

S. Apollinare Nuovo: Shell-shaped decorative panel

S. Apollinare Nuovo: Christ before Pilate

S. Apollinare Nuovo: The announcement of Peter's denial

S. Apollinare Nuovo: The announcement of Peter's denial (detail)

S. Apollinare Nuovo: Christ going into Calvary 105

S. Apollinare Nuovo: *The pious women at the Tomb*

S. Apollinare Nuovo:
*Jesus before
the Synedrion*

106

S. Apollinare in Classe: The Apse

*S. Apollinare
in Classe:
Interior* ⟁

SALVS MVNDI

S. Apollinare in Classe: The cross in the apsis conch

S. Apollinare in Classe: The sacrifice of Abel, Melchizedek and Abraham

S. Apollinare in Classe: Detail of the mosaics of the apsis conch

S. Apollinare in Classe:
The apsis (detail)

S. Apollinare in Classe:
The apsis (detail)

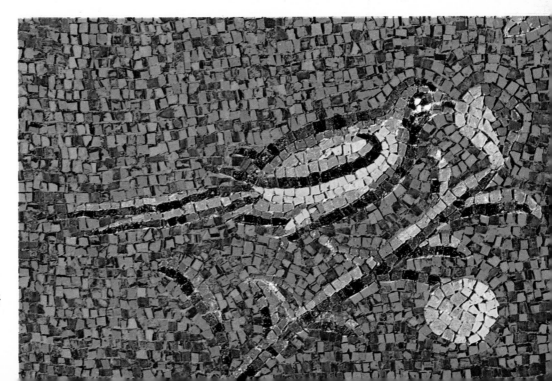

Apollinare in Classe:
he apsis (detail)

Archbishop's Chapel: Interior of the oratory

The Archbishop's Chapel: the vault

Archbishop's Chapel:
Decoration
of the vault (detail)

EGO VERI
SVM ITAS ET
VIA VITA

Archbishop's Chapel:
Jesus Christ
as a warrior

Archiepiscopal Museum:
Bishop Ursicinus

Archiepiscopal Museum:
Mosaic from the ancient Cathedra

Archiepiscopal Museum:
Bishop Barbatianus

The Archiepiscopal Museum: ivory throne of Maximian

Archiepiscopal Museum:
Ivory throne of Maximian (detail)

Archiepiscopal Museum:
Ivory throne of Maximian (detail)

The Archiepiscopal Museum: ivory throne (detail)

National Museum:
The diptych of Murano (ivory, 6 th cent.)

National Museum:
Relief with Hercules and deer
(5th cent.)

Academy Gallery: St. Peter Damiani
(Giovanni Antonio da Pesaro, 15th cent.)

Academy Gallery:
Guidarello Guidarelli

Academy Gallery:
The Crucifixion
by Antonio Vivarini
(15th cent.)

The Cathedral: Interior

The Cathedral:
Fresco by Guido Reni

S. Maria in Porto

S. Giovanni Evangelista

ILLUSTRATIONS INDEX